D0597061

The Crusades
and the Holy Wars

FABRICE ERRE
Writer

SYLVAIN SAVOIA
Artist

PAPERCUTZ™

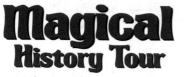

Magical History Tour

#4 "The Crusades and the Holy Wars"

By Fabrice Erre and Sylvain Savoia

Original series editors: Frédéric Niffle and Lewis Trondheim
Translation: Joseph Laredo
Lettering: Cromatik Ltd

Jeff Whitman – Managing Editor
Jim Salicrup
Editor-in-Chief

ISBN 978-1-5458-0714-9

Originally published in French as *"Le Fil de l'Histoire – Les Croisades. Conflicts en Terre Sainte"*

www.papercutz.com

Papercutz books may be purchased for business or promotional use. For information on bulk purchases please contact Macmillan Corporate and Premium Sales Department at (800) 221-7945 x5442.

Printed in Malaysia
August 2021

Distributed by Macmillan
First Printing

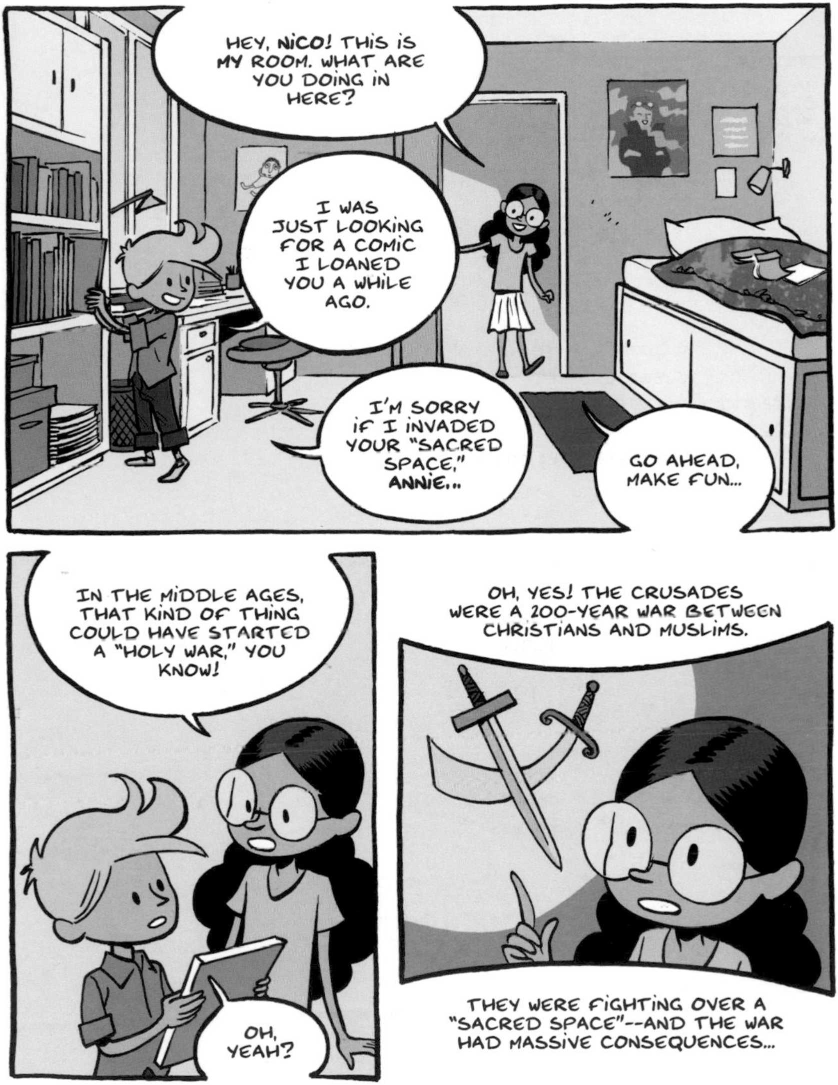
HEY, NICO! THIS IS MY ROOM. WHAT ARE YOU DOING IN HERE?
I WAS JUST LOOKING FOR A COMIC I LOANED YOU A WHILE AGO.
I'M SORRY IF I INVADED YOUR "SACRED SPACE," ANNIE...
GO AHEAD, MAKE FUN...
IN THE MIDDLE AGES, THAT KIND OF THING COULD HAVE STARTED A "HOLY WAR," YOU KNOW!
OH, YEAH?
OH, YES! THE CRUSADES WERE A 200-YEAR WAR BETWEEN CHRISTIANS AND MUSLIMS.
THEY WERE FIGHTING OVER A "SACRED SPACE"--AND THE WAR HAD MASSIVE CONSEQUENCES...

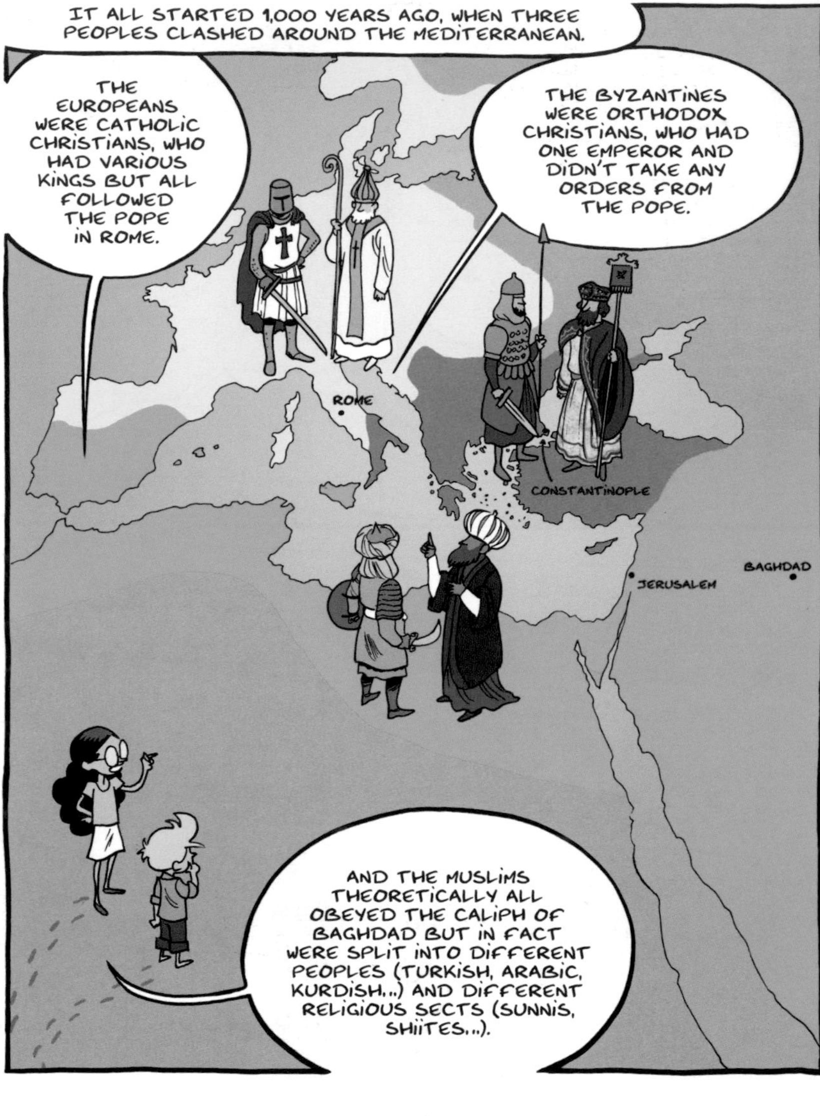
IT ALL STARTED 1,000 YEARS AGO, WHEN THREE PEOPLES CLASHED AROUND THE MEDITERRANEAN.
THE EUROPEANS WERE CATHOLIC CHRISTIANS, WHO HAD VARIOUS KINGS BUT ALL FOLLOWED THE POPE IN ROME.
THE BYZANTINES WERE ORTHODOX CHRISTIANS, WHO HAD ONE EMPEROR AND DIDN'T TAKE ANY ORDERS FROM THE POPE.
ROME
CONSTANTINOPLE
BAGHDAD
JERUSALEM
AND THE MUSLIMS THEORETICALLY ALL OBEYED THE CALIPH OF BAGHDAD BUT IN FACT WERE SPLIT INTO DIFFERENT PEOPLES (TURKISH, ARABIC, KURDISH...) AND DIFFERENT RELIGIOUS SECTS (SUNNIS, SHIITES...).

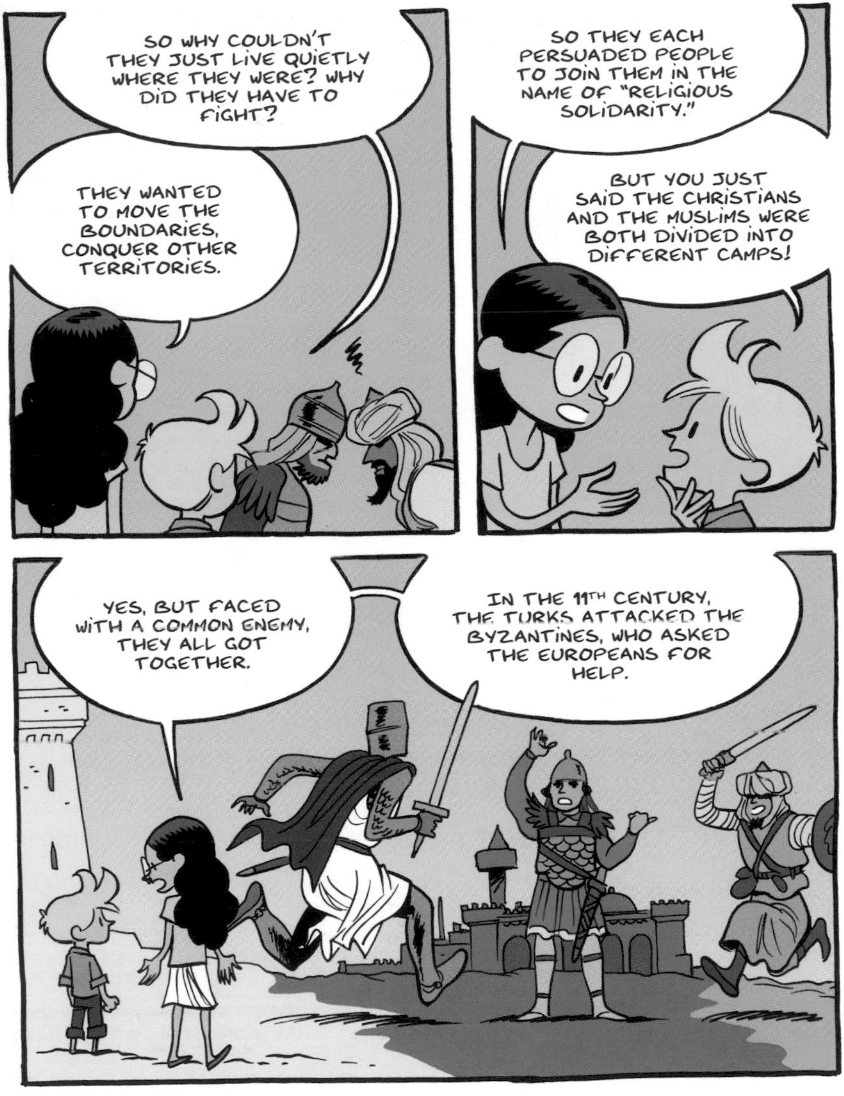
SO WHY COULDN'T THEY JUST LIVE QUIETLY WHERE THEY WERE? WHY DID THEY HAVE TO FIGHT?
THEY WANTED TO MOVE THE BOUNDARIES, CONQUER OTHER TERRITORIES.
SO THEY EACH PERSUADED PEOPLE TO JOIN THEM IN THE NAME OF "RELIGIOUS SOLIDARITY."
BUT YOU JUST SAID THE CHRISTIANS AND THE MUSLIMS WERE BOTH DIVIDED INTO DIFFERENT CAMPS!
YES, BUT FACED WITH A COMMON ENEMY, THEY ALL GOT TOGETHER.
IN THE 11TH CENTURY, THE TURKS ATTACKED THE BYZANTINES, WHO ASKED THE EUROPEANS FOR HELP.

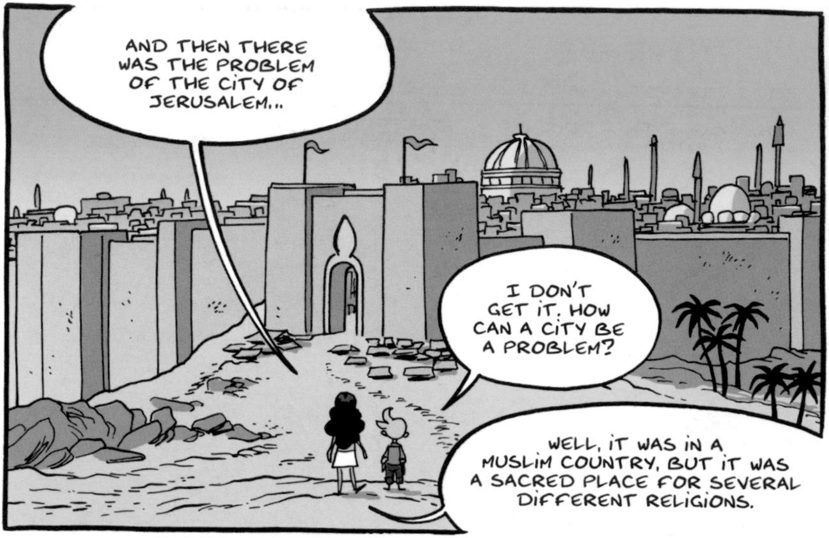
AND THEN THERE WAS THE PROBLEM OF THE CITY OF JERUSALEM...
I DON'T GET IT. HOW CAN A CITY BE A PROBLEM?
WELL, IT WAS IN A MUSLIM COUNTRY, BUT IT WAS A SACRED PLACE FOR SEVERAL DIFFERENT RELIGIONS.

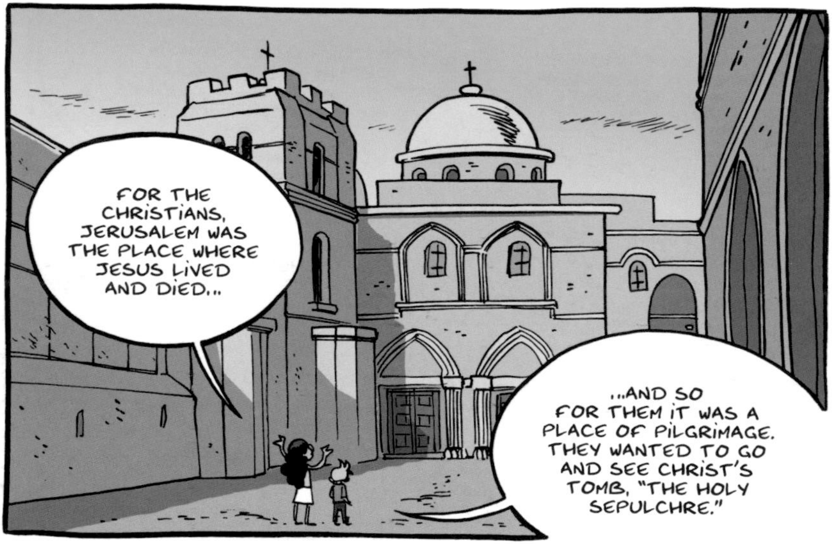
FOR THE CHRISTIANS, JERUSALEM WAS THE PLACE WHERE JESUS LIVED AND DIED...
...AND SO FOR THEM IT WAS A PLACE OF PILGRIMAGE. THEY WANTED TO GO AND SEE CHRIST'S TOMB, "THE HOLY SEPULCHRE."

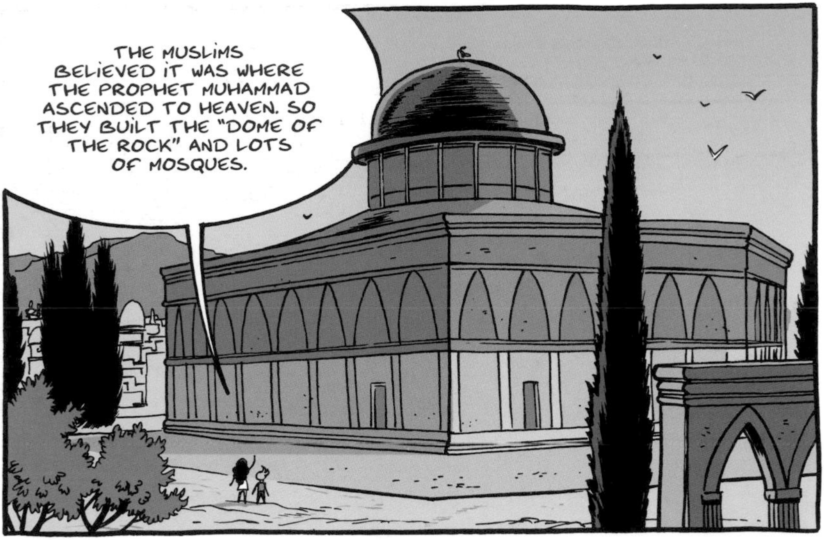
THE MUSLIMS BELIEVED IT WAS WHERE THE PROPHET MUHAMMAD ASCENDED TO HEAVEN. SO THEY BUILT THE "DOME OF THE ROCK" AND LOTS OF MOSQUES.

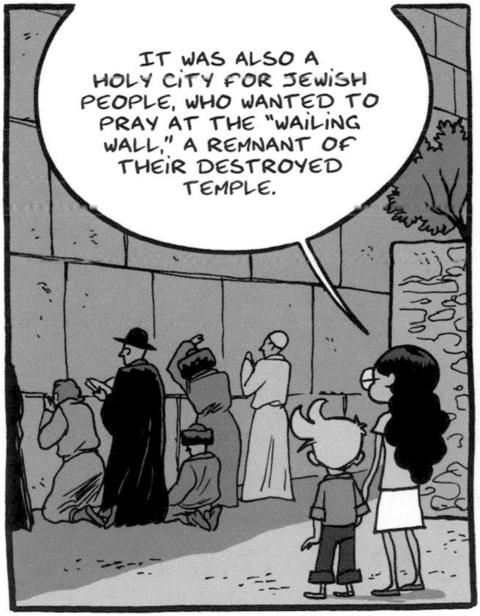
IT WAS ALSO A HOLY CITY FOR JEWISH PEOPLE, WHO WANTED TO PRAY AT THE "WAILING WALL," A REMNANT OF THEIR DESTROYED TEMPLE.

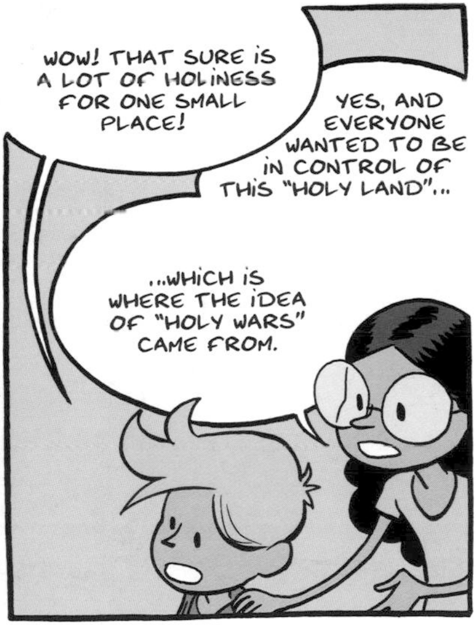
WOW! THAT SURE IS A LOT OF HOLINESS FOR ONE SMALL PLACE!
YES, AND EVERYONE WANTED TO BE IN CONTROL OF THIS "HOLY LAND"...
...WHICH IS WHERE THE IDEA OF "HOLY WARS" CAME FROM.

IN 1071, THE TURKS TOOK CONTROL OF JERUSALEM AND STOPPED THE CHRISTIANS FROM GOING THERE, WHICH MADE THE CHRISTIAN KNIGHTS FURIOUS. SO IN 1095, **POPE URBAN II** WENT TO CLERMONT-FERRAND IN FRANCE TO LAUNCH AN APPEAL TO ALL EUROPEANS TO GO FIGHT THE TURKISH "INFIDELS."

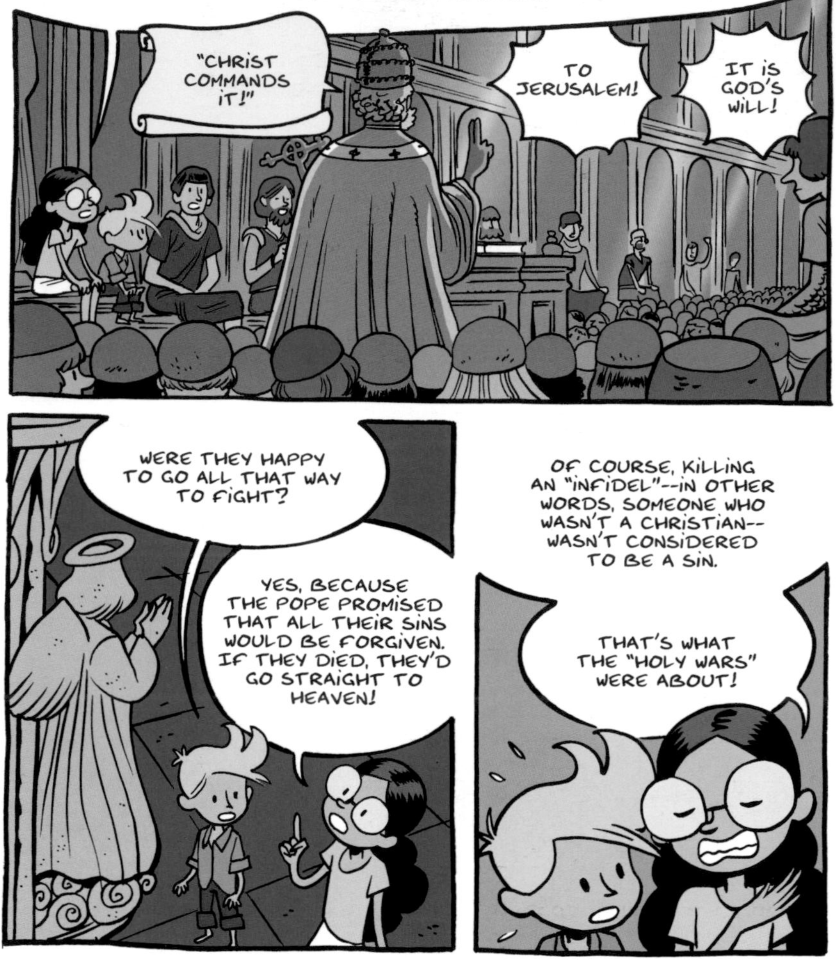
"CHRIST COMMANDS IT!"
TO JERUSALEM!
IT IS GOD'S WILL!
WERE THEY HAPPY TO GO ALL THAT WAY TO FIGHT?
YES, BECAUSE THE POPE PROMISED THAT ALL THEIR SINS WOULD BE FORGIVEN. IF THEY DIED, THEY'D GO STRAIGHT TO HEAVEN!
OF COURSE, KILLING AN "INFIDEL"--IN OTHER WORDS, SOMEONE WHO WASN'T A CHRISTIAN--WASN'T CONSIDERED TO BE A SIN.
THAT'S WHAT THE "HOLY WARS" WERE ABOUT!

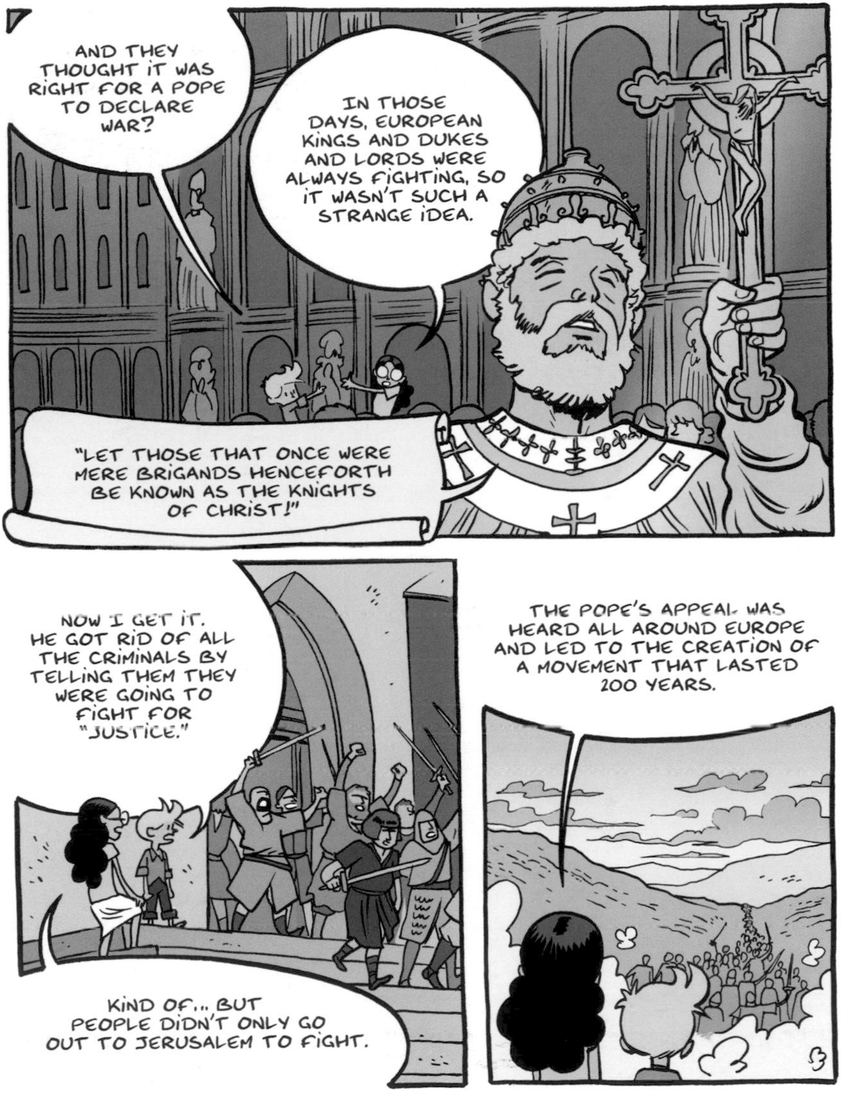
AND THEY THOUGHT IT WAS RIGHT FOR A POPE TO DECLARE WAR?
IN THOSE DAYS, EUROPEAN KINGS AND DUKES AND LORDS WERE ALWAYS FIGHTING, SO IT WASN'T SUCH A STRANGE IDEA.
"LET THOSE THAT ONCE WERE MERE BRIGANDS HENCEFORTH BE KNOWN AS THE KNIGHTS OF CHRIST!"
NOW I GET IT. HE GOT RID OF ALL THE CRIMINALS BY TELLING THEM THEY WERE GOING TO FIGHT FOR "JUSTICE."
KIND OF... BUT PEOPLE DIDN'T ONLY GO OUT TO JERUSALEM TO FIGHT.
THE POPE'S APPEAL WAS HEARD ALL AROUND EUROPE AND LED TO THE CREATION OF A MOVEMENT THAT LASTED 200 YEARS.

THE FIRST JOURNEY TO JERUSALEM WAS IN 1096. EVERYONE PAINTED A CROSS ON THEIR CLOTHES--SO IT BECAME KNOWN AS A "CRUSADE," FROM THE WORD "CROSS."

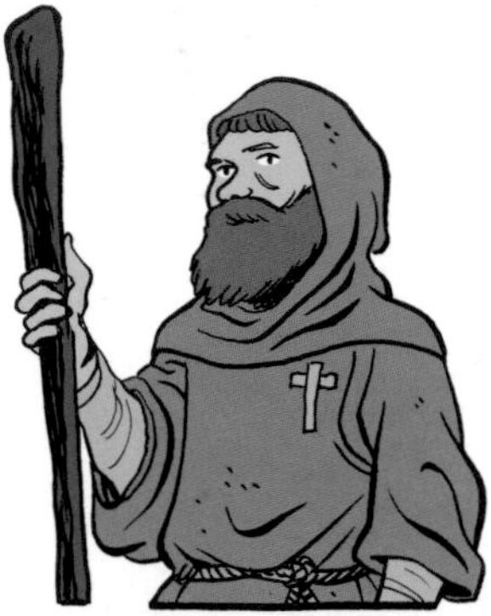

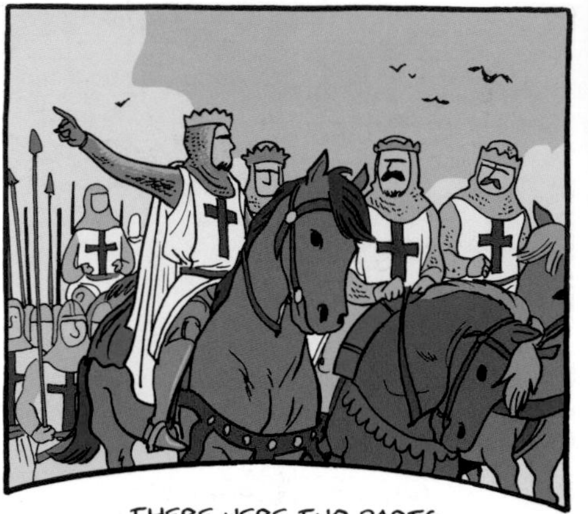

THERE WERE TWO PARTS TO IT: "THE PRINCES' CRUSADE," LED BY NOBLEMEN SUCH AS **GODFREY OF BOUILLON**, A DUKE FROM EASTERN FRANCE...

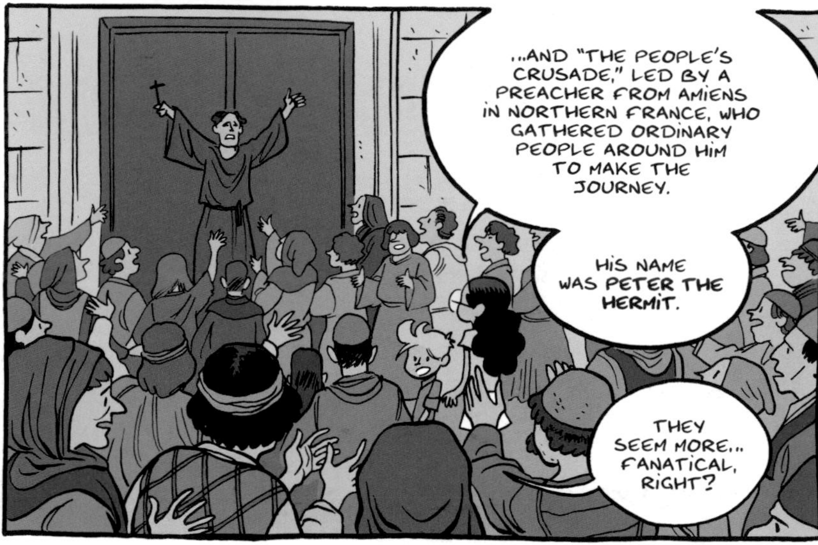
...AND "THE PEOPLE'S CRUSADE," LED BY A PREACHER FROM AMIENS IN NORTHERN FRANCE, WHO GATHERED ORDINARY PEOPLE AROUND HIM TO MAKE THE JOURNEY.
HIS NAME WAS **PETER THE HERMIT**.
THEY SEEM MORE... FANATICAL, RIGHT?

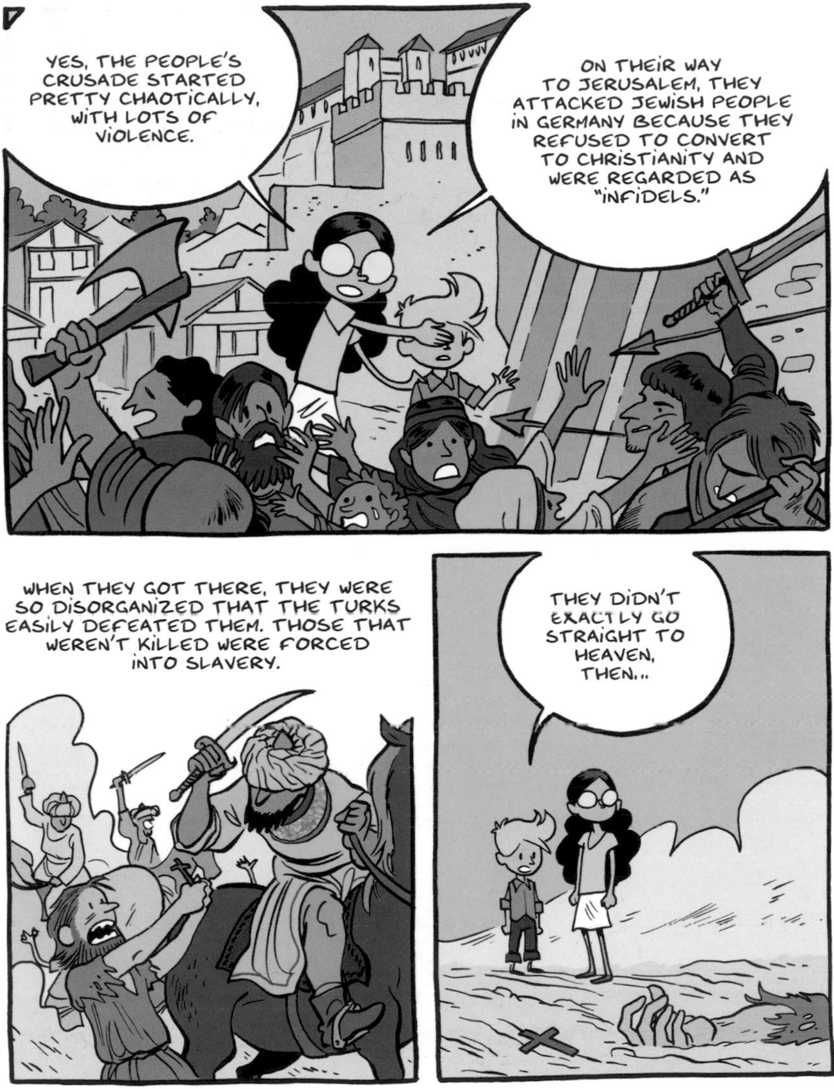
YES, THE PEOPLE'S CRUSADE STARTED PRETTY CHAOTICALLY, WITH LOTS OF VIOLENCE.
ON THEIR WAY TO JERUSALEM, THEY ATTACKED JEWISH PEOPLE IN GERMANY BECAUSE THEY REFUSED TO CONVERT TO CHRISTIANITY AND WERE REGARDED AS "INFIDELS."
WHEN THEY GOT THERE, THEY WERE SO DISORGANIZED THAT THE TURKS EASILY DEFEATED THEM. THOSE THAT WEREN'T KILLED WERE FORCED INTO SLAVERY.
THEY DIDN'T EXACTLY GO STRAIGHT TO HEAVEN, THEN...

THE PRINCES' CRUSADE WAS BETTER PREPARED. SUDDENLY, THE TURKS WERE FACING 100,000 SOLIDERS, BACKED BY THE BYZANTINE EMPEROR.

THE CRUSADERS TOOK SEVERAL CITIES, CLAIMING THAT GOD WAS ON THEIR SIDE. IT'S SAID THAT GODFREY OF BOUILLON SLICED A TURK IN HALF WITH A SINGLE SWIPE OF HIS SWORD!

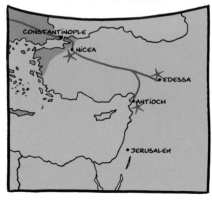

CONSTANTINOPLE

NICEA

EDESSA

ANTIOCH

JERUSALEM

REALLY?

LET'S JUST SAY IT WAS MAINLY A CASE OF THE CRUSADERS HAVING BETTER ARMOR.

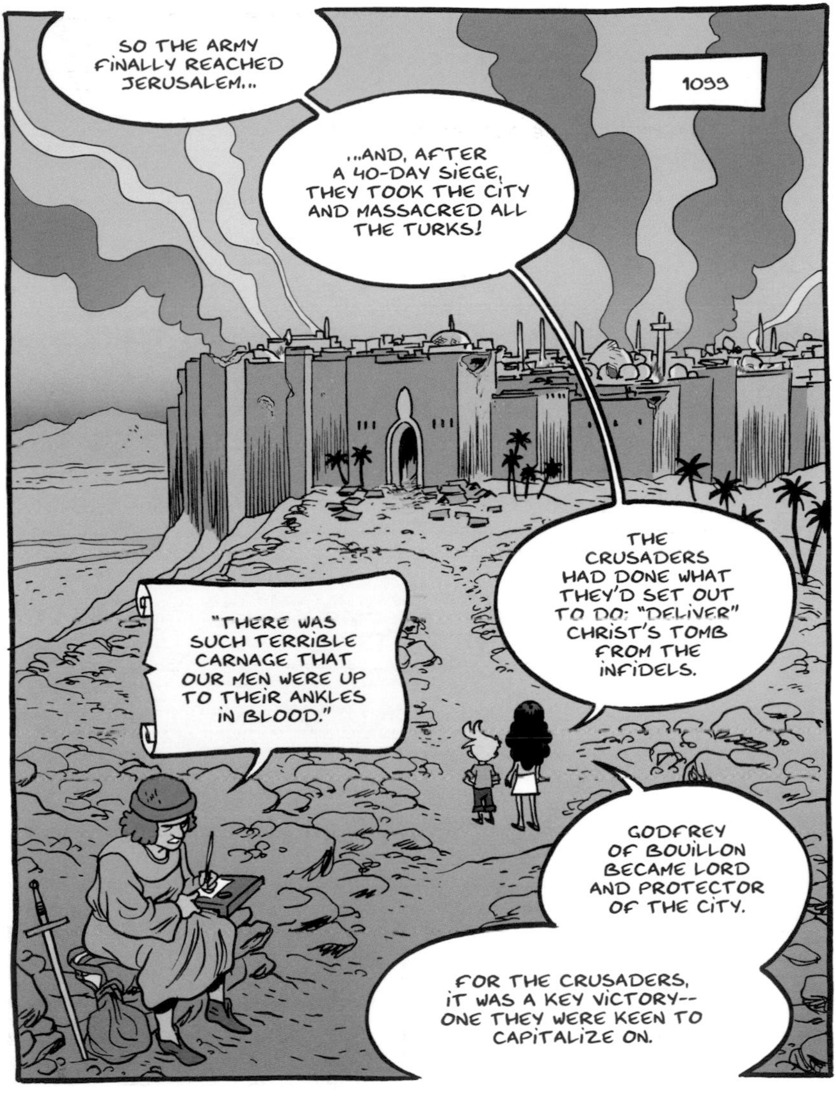
SO THE ARMY FINALLY REACHED JERUSALEM...
1099
...AND, AFTER A 40-DAY SIEGE, THEY TOOK THE CITY AND MASSACRED ALL THE TURKS!
THE CRUSADERS HAD DONE WHAT THEY'D SET OUT TO DO: "DELIVER" CHRIST'S TOMB FROM THE INFIDELS.
"THERE WAS SUCH TERRIBLE CARNAGE THAT OUR MEN WERE UP TO THEIR ANKLES IN BLOOD."
GODFREY OF BOUILLON BECAME LORD AND PROTECTOR OF THE CITY.
FOR THE CRUSADERS, IT WAS A KEY VICTORY--ONE THEY WERE KEEN TO CAPITALIZE ON.

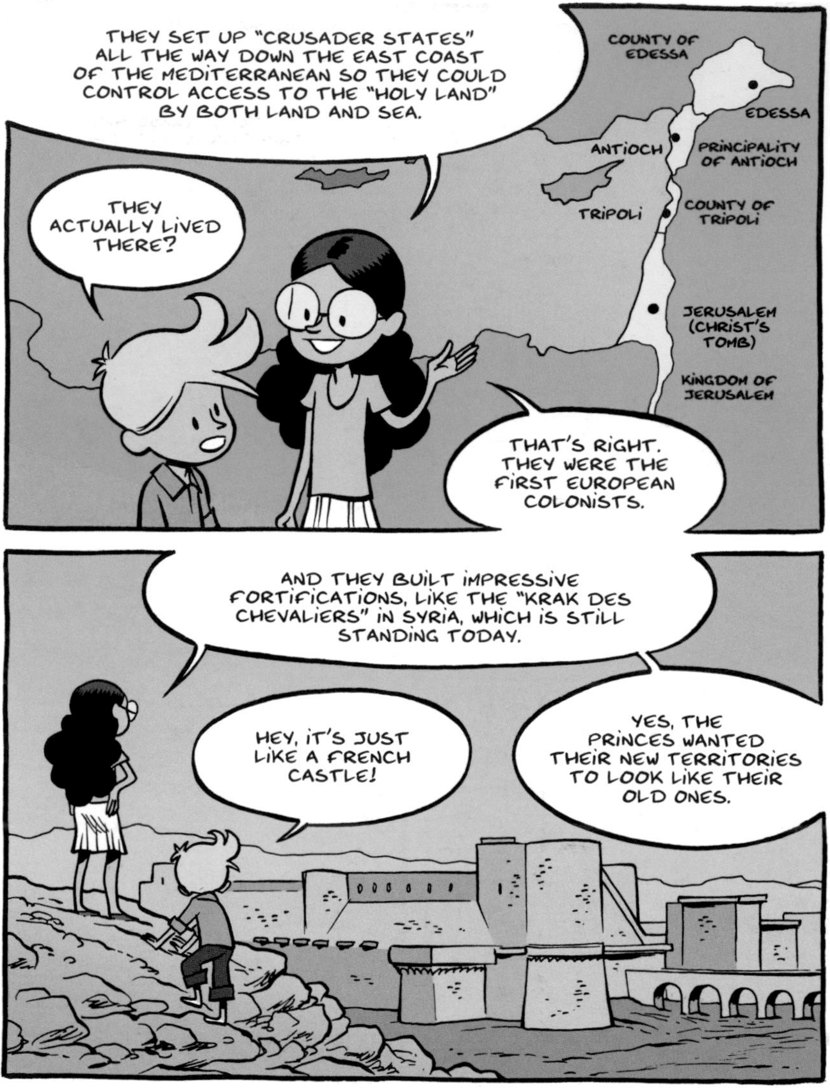
THEY SET UP "CRUSADER STATES" ALL THE WAY DOWN THE EAST COAST OF THE MEDITERRANEAN SO THEY COULD CONTROL ACCESS TO THE "HOLY LAND" BY BOTH LAND AND SEA.
COUNTY OF EDESSA
EDESSA
ANTIOCH
PRINCIPALITY OF ANTIOCH
TRIPOLI
COUNTY OF TRIPOLI
JERUSALEM (CHRIST'S TOMB)
KINGDOM OF JERUSALEM
THEY ACTUALLY LIVED THERE?
THAT'S RIGHT. THEY WERE THE FIRST EUROPEAN COLONISTS.
AND THEY BUILT IMPRESSIVE FORTIFICATIONS, LIKE THE "KRAK DES CHEVALIERS" IN SYRIA, WHICH IS STILL STANDING TODAY.
HEY, IT'S JUST LIKE A FRENCH CASTLE!
YES, THE PRINCES WANTED THEIR NEW TERRITORIES TO LOOK LIKE THEIR OLD ONES.

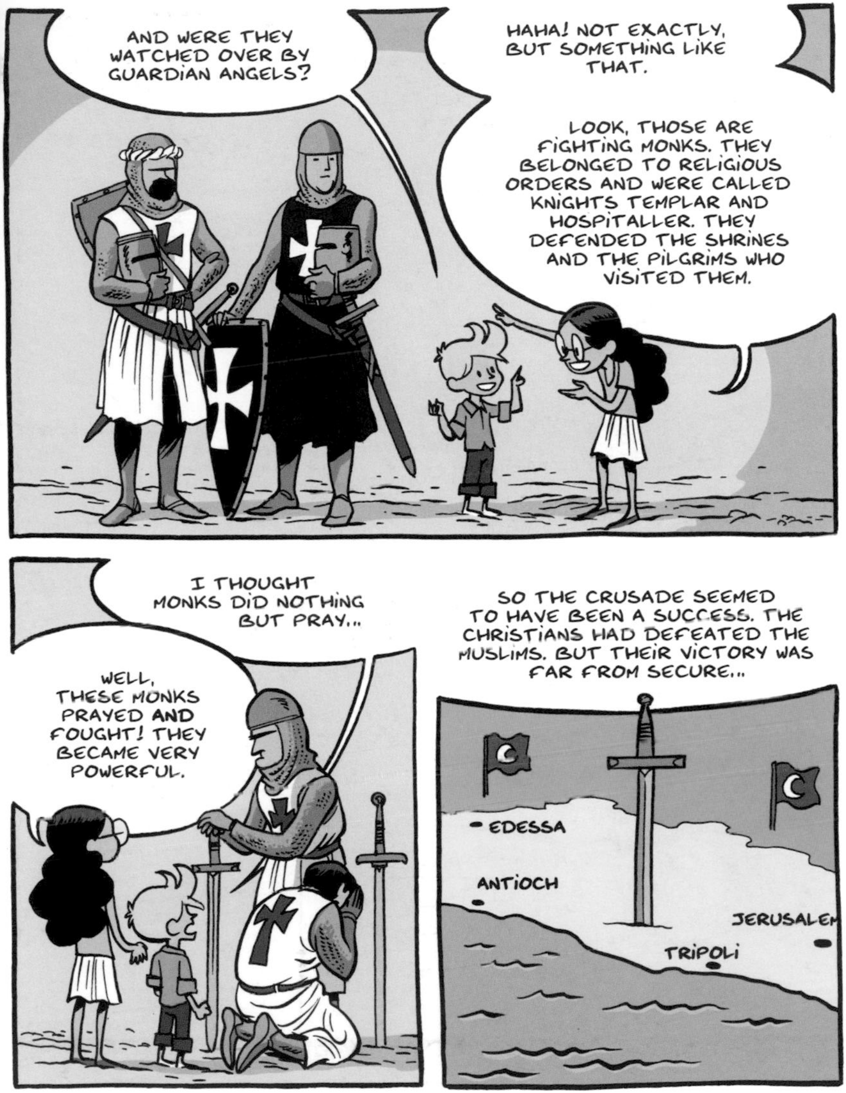
AND WERE THEY WATCHED OVER BY GUARDIAN ANGELS?
HAHA! NOT EXACTLY, BUT SOMETHING LIKE THAT.
LOOK, THOSE ARE FIGHTING MONKS. THEY BELONGED TO RELIGIOUS ORDERS AND WERE CALLED KNIGHTS TEMPLAR AND HOSPITALLER. THEY DEFENDED THE SHRINES AND THE PILGRIMS WHO VISITED THEM.
I THOUGHT MONKS DID NOTHING BUT PRAY...
WELL, THESE MONKS PRAYED AND FOUGHT! THEY BECAME VERY POWERFUL.
SO THE CRUSADE SEEMED TO HAVE BEEN A SUCCESS. THE CHRISTIANS HAD DEFEATED THE MUSLIMS. BUT THEIR VICTORY WAS FAR FROM SECURE...
EDESSA
ANTIOCH
JERUSALEM
TRIPOLI

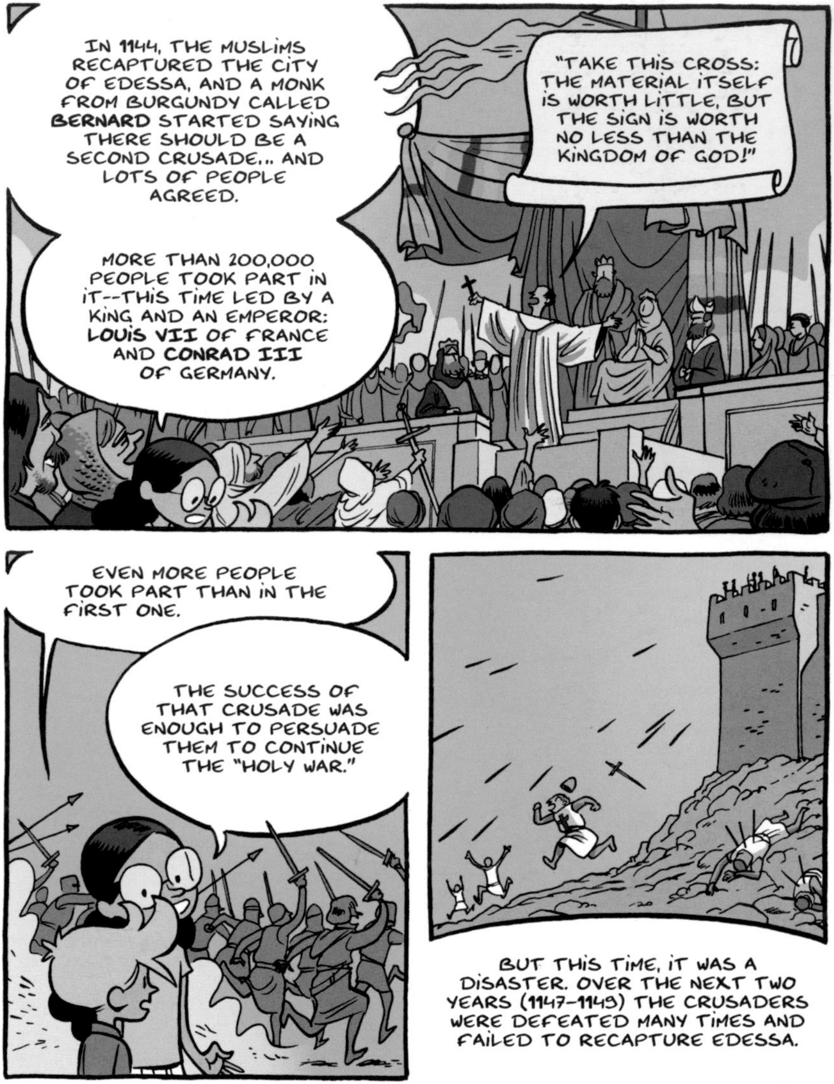
IN 1144, THE MUSLIMS RECAPTURED THE CITY OF EDESSA, AND A MONK FROM BURGUNDY CALLED **BERNARD** STARTED SAYING THERE SHOULD BE A SECOND CRUSADE... AND LOTS OF PEOPLE AGREED.
"TAKE THIS CROSS: THE MATERIAL ITSELF IS WORTH LITTLE, BUT THE SIGN IS WORTH NO LESS THAN THE KINGDOM OF GOD!"
MORE THAN 200,000 PEOPLE TOOK PART IN IT--THIS TIME LED BY A KING AND AN EMPEROR: **LOUIS VII** OF FRANCE AND **CONRAD III** OF GERMANY.
EVEN MORE PEOPLE TOOK PART THAN IN THE FIRST ONE.
THE SUCCESS OF THAT CRUSADE WAS ENOUGH TO PERSUADE THEM TO CONTINUE THE "HOLY WAR."
BUT THIS TIME, IT WAS A DISASTER. OVER THE NEXT TWO YEARS (1147–1149) THE CRUSADERS WERE DEFEATED MANY TIMES AND FAILED TO RECAPTURE EDESSA.

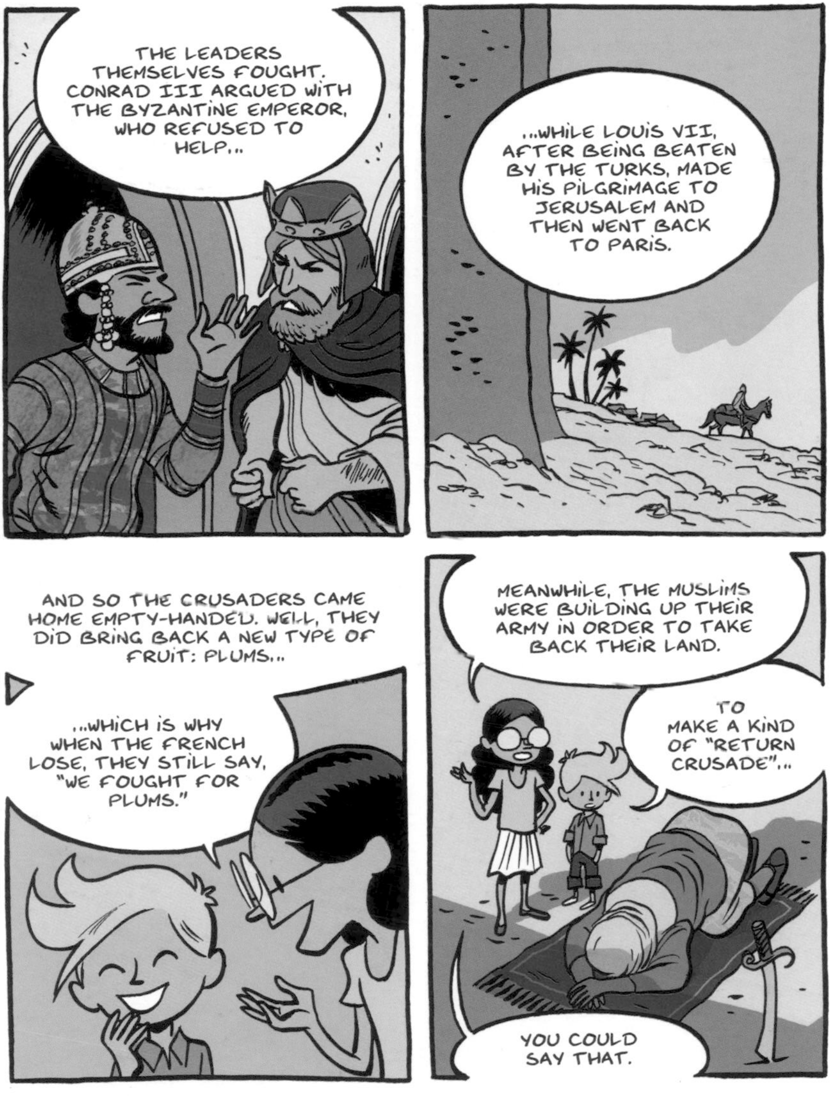
THE LEADERS THEMSELVES FOUGHT. CONRAD III ARGUED WITH THE BYZANTINE EMPEROR, WHO REFUSED TO HELP...
...WHILE LOUIS VII, AFTER BEING BEATEN BY THE TURKS, MADE HIS PILGRIMAGE TO JERUSALEM AND THEN WENT BACK TO PARIS.
AND SO THE CRUSADERS CAME HOME EMPTY-HANDED. WELL, THEY DID BRING BACK A NEW TYPE OF FRUIT: PLUMS...
...WHICH IS WHY WHEN THE FRENCH LOSE, THEY STILL SAY, "WE FOUGHT FOR PLUMS."
MEANWHILE, THE MUSLIMS WERE BUILDING UP THEIR ARMY IN ORDER TO TAKE BACK THEIR LAND.
TO MAKE A KIND OF "RETURN CRUSADE"...
YOU COULD SAY THAT.

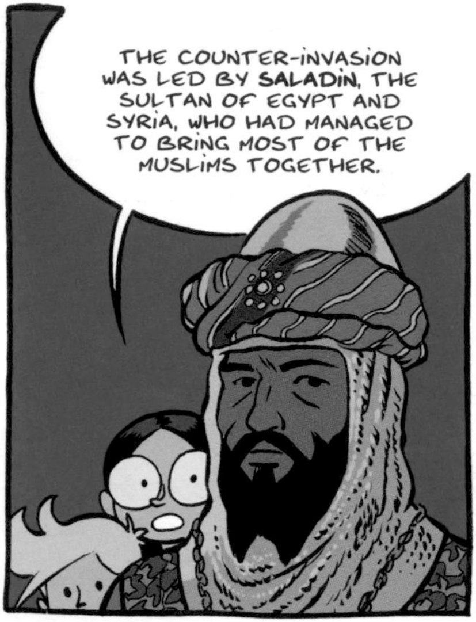
THE COUNTER-INVASION WAS LED BY **SALADIN**, THE SULTAN OF EGYPT AND SYRIA, WHO HAD MANAGED TO BRING MOST OF THE MUSLIMS TOGETHER.

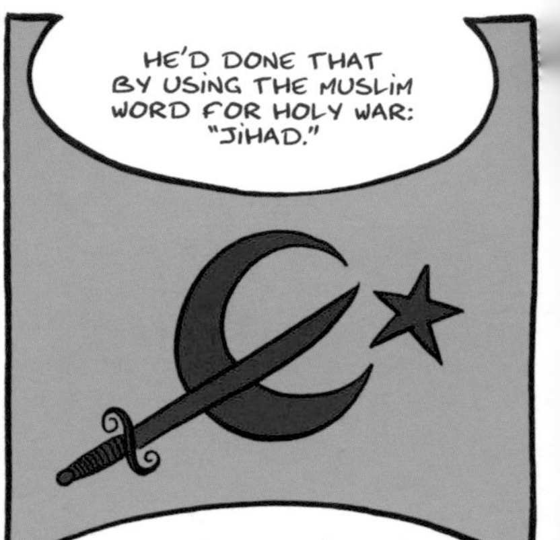
HE'D DONE THAT BY USING THE MUSLIM WORD FOR HOLY WAR: "JIHAD."

THE WORD "JIHAD" REFERS TO THE "STRUGGLE" TO FOLLOW ISLAM, BUT SALADIN GAVE IT A WARLIKE MEANING: THE FIGHT AGAINST THE CRUSADERS, THE "INFIDELS."

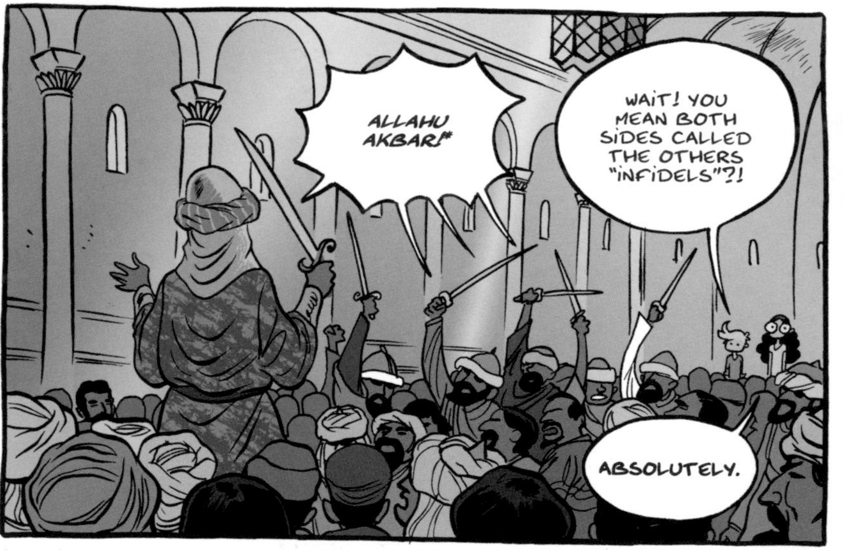
*ALLAHU AKBAR!**
WAIT! YOU MEAN BOTH SIDES CALLED THE OTHERS "INFIDELS"?!
ABSOLUTELY.

*GOD (ALLAH) IS MOST GREAT.

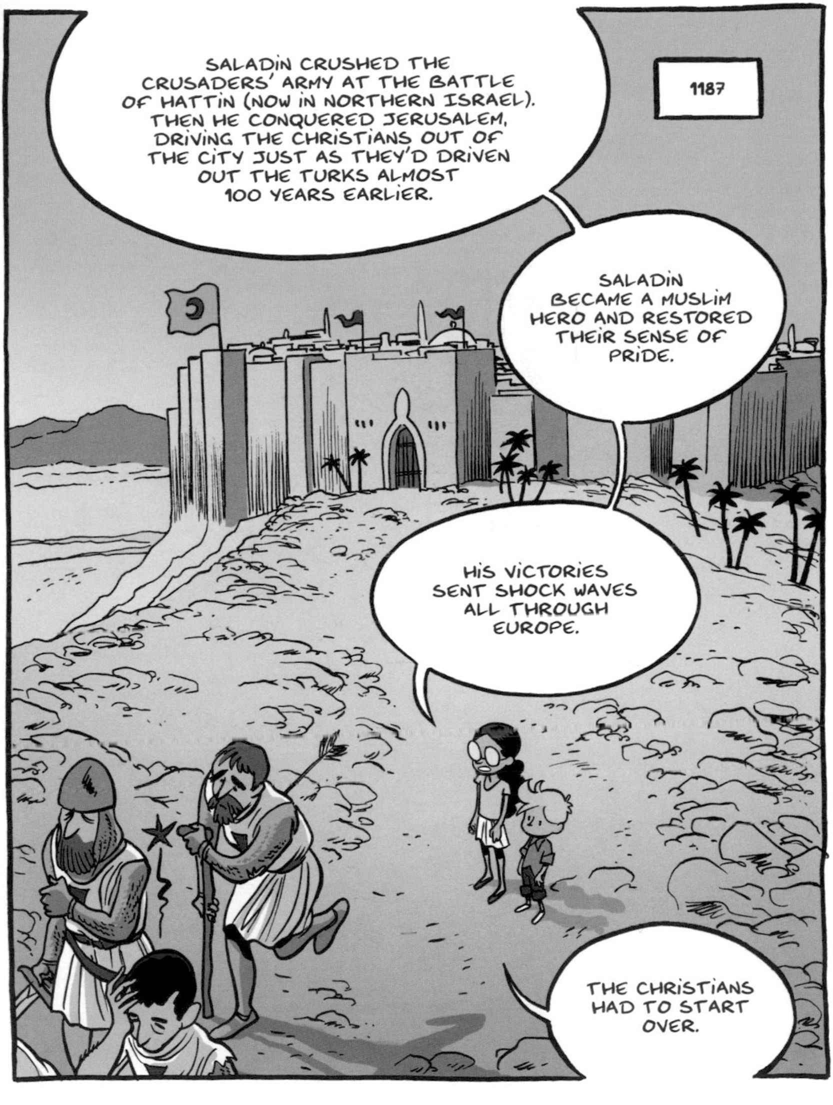
1187
SALADIN CRUSHED THE CRUSADERS' ARMY AT THE BATTLE OF HATTIN (NOW IN NORTHERN ISRAEL). THEN HE CONQUERED JERUSALEM, DRIVING THE CHRISTIANS OUT OF THE CITY JUST AS THEY'D DRIVEN OUT THE TURKS ALMOST 100 YEARS EARLIER.
SALADIN BECAME A MUSLIM HERO AND RESTORED THEIR SENSE OF PRIDE.
HIS VICTORIES SENT SHOCK WAVES ALL THROUGH EUROPE.
THE CHRISTIANS HAD TO START OVER.

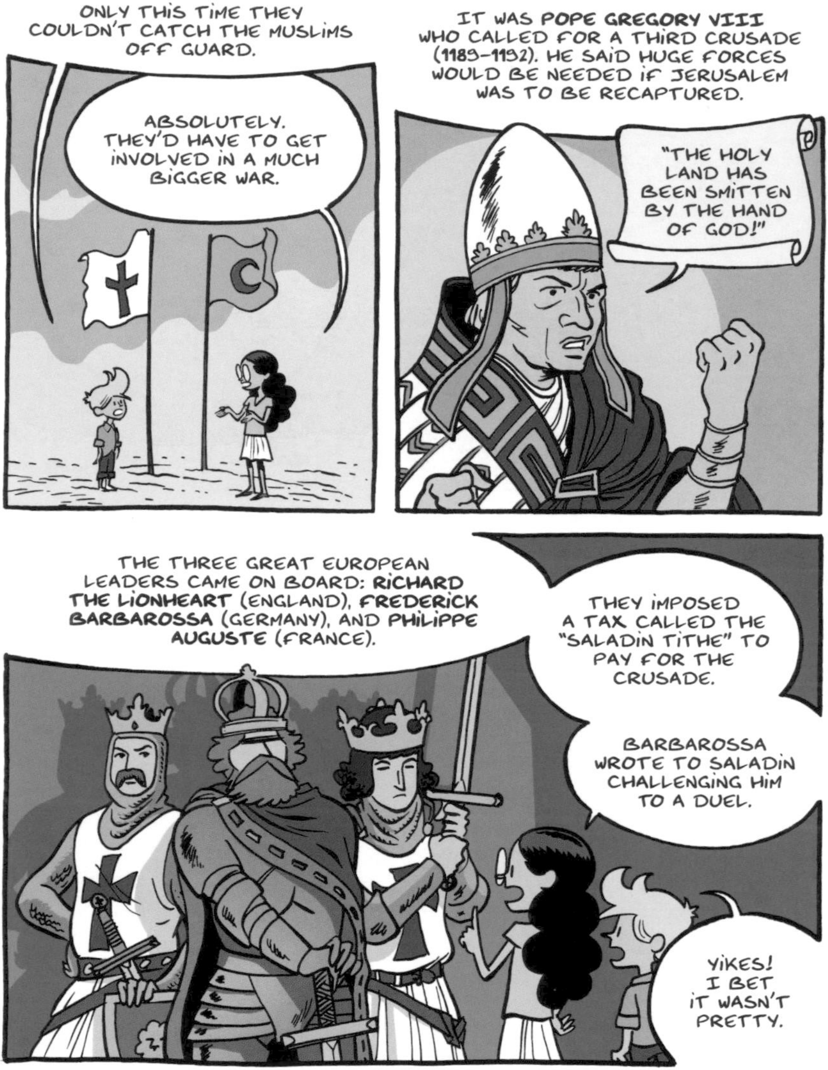
ONLY THIS TIME THEY COULDN'T CATCH THE MUSLIMS OFF GUARD.
ABSOLUTELY. THEY'D HAVE TO GET INVOLVED IN A MUCH BIGGER WAR.
IT WAS **POPE GREGORY VIII** WHO CALLED FOR A THIRD CRUSADE (1189–1192). HE SAID HUGE FORCES WOULD BE NEEDED IF JERUSALEM WAS TO BE RECAPTURED.
"THE HOLY LAND HAS BEEN SMITTEN BY THE HAND OF GOD!"
THE THREE GREAT EUROPEAN LEADERS CAME ON BOARD: **RICHARD THE LIONHEART** (ENGLAND), **FREDERICK BARBAROSSA** (GERMANY), AND **PHILIPPE AUGUSTE** (FRANCE).
THEY IMPOSED A TAX CALLED THE "SALADIN TITHE" TO PAY FOR THE CRUSADE.
BARBAROSSA WROTE TO SALADIN CHALLENGING HIM TO A DUEL.
YIKES! I BET IT WASN'T PRETTY.

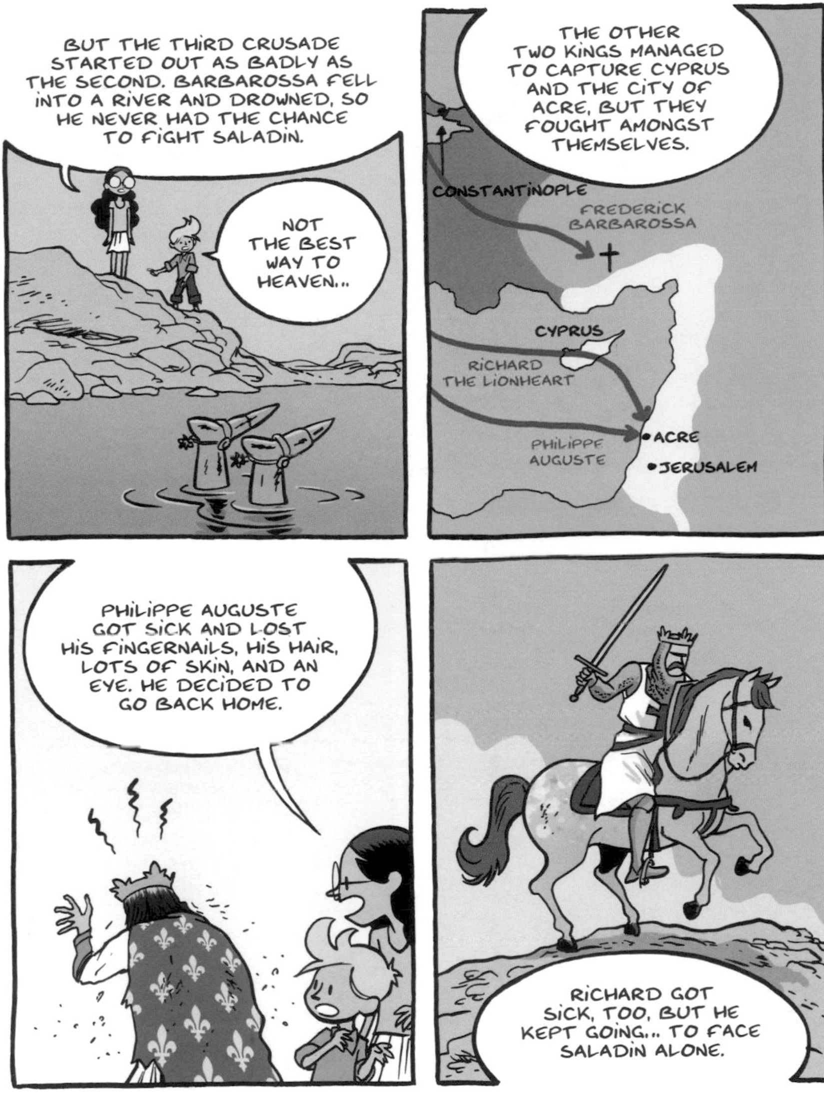
BUT THE THIRD CRUSADE STARTED OUT AS BADLY AS THE SECOND. BARBAROSSA FELL INTO A RIVER AND DROWNED, SO HE NEVER HAD THE CHANCE TO FIGHT SALADIN.
NOT THE BEST WAY TO HEAVEN...
THE OTHER TWO KINGS MANAGED TO CAPTURE CYPRUS AND THE CITY OF ACRE, BUT THEY FOUGHT AMONGST THEMSELVES.
CONSTANTINOPLE
FREDERICK BARBAROSSA
CYPRUS
RICHARD THE LIONHEART
PHILIPPE AUGUSTE
ACRE
JERUSALEM
PHILIPPE AUGUSTE GOT SICK AND LOST HIS FINGERNAILS, HIS HAIR, LOTS OF SKIN, AND AN EYE. HE DECIDED TO GO BACK HOME.
RICHARD GOT SICK, TOO, BUT HE KEPT GOING... TO FACE SALADIN ALONE.

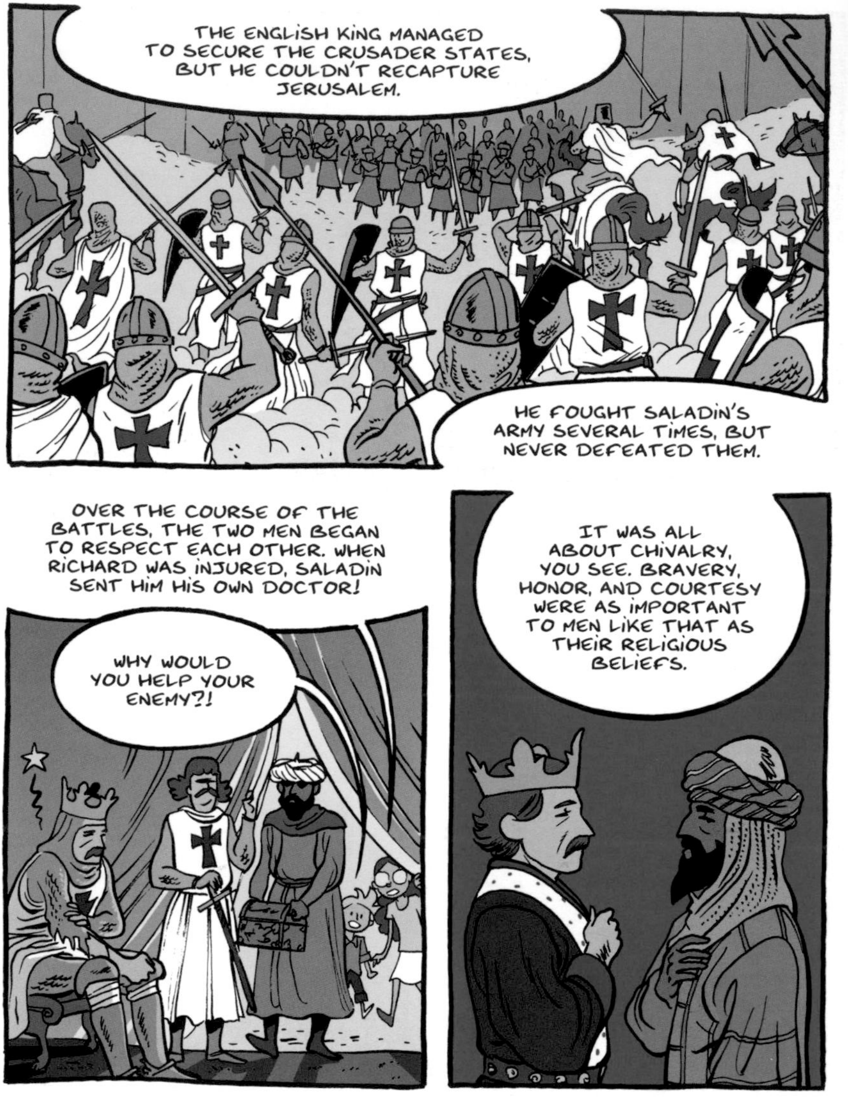
THE ENGLISH KING MANAGED TO SECURE THE CRUSADER STATES, BUT HE COULDN'T RECAPTURE JERUSALEM.
HE FOUGHT SALADIN'S ARMY SEVERAL TIMES, BUT NEVER DEFEATED THEM.
OVER THE COURSE OF THE BATTLES, THE TWO MEN BEGAN TO RESPECT EACH OTHER. WHEN RICHARD WAS INJURED, SALADIN SENT HIM HIS OWN DOCTOR!
WHY WOULD YOU HELP YOUR ENEMY?!
IT WAS ALL ABOUT CHIVALRY, YOU SEE. BRAVERY, HONOR, AND COURTESY WERE AS IMPORTANT TO MEN LIKE THAT AS THEIR RELIGIOUS BELIEFS.

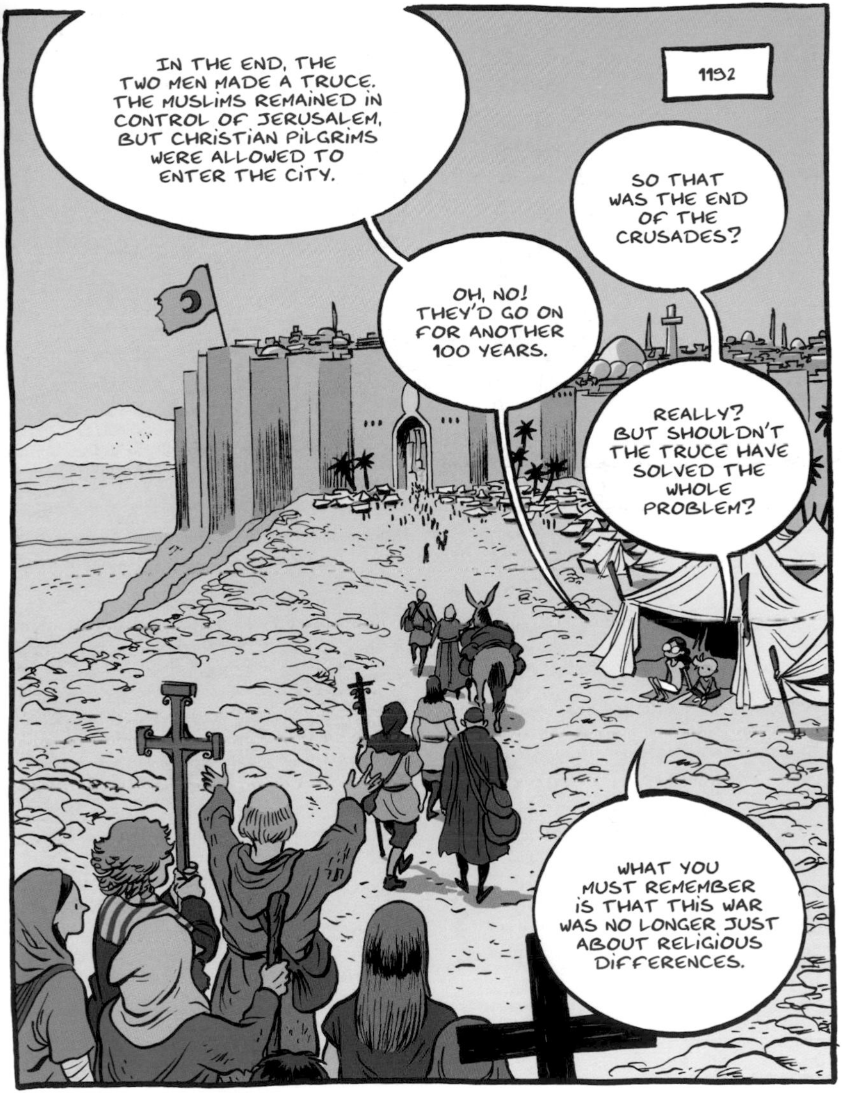
IN THE END, THE TWO MEN MADE A TRUCE. THE MUSLIMS REMAINED IN CONTROL OF JERUSALEM, BUT CHRISTIAN PILGRIMS WERE ALLOWED TO ENTER THE CITY.
1192
SO THAT WAS THE END OF THE CRUSADES?
OH, NO! THEY'D GO ON FOR ANOTHER 100 YEARS.
REALLY? BUT SHOULDN'T THE TRUCE HAVE SOLVED THE WHOLE PROBLEM?
WHAT YOU MUST REMEMBER IS THAT THIS WAR WAS NO LONGER JUST ABOUT RELIGIOUS DIFFERENCES.

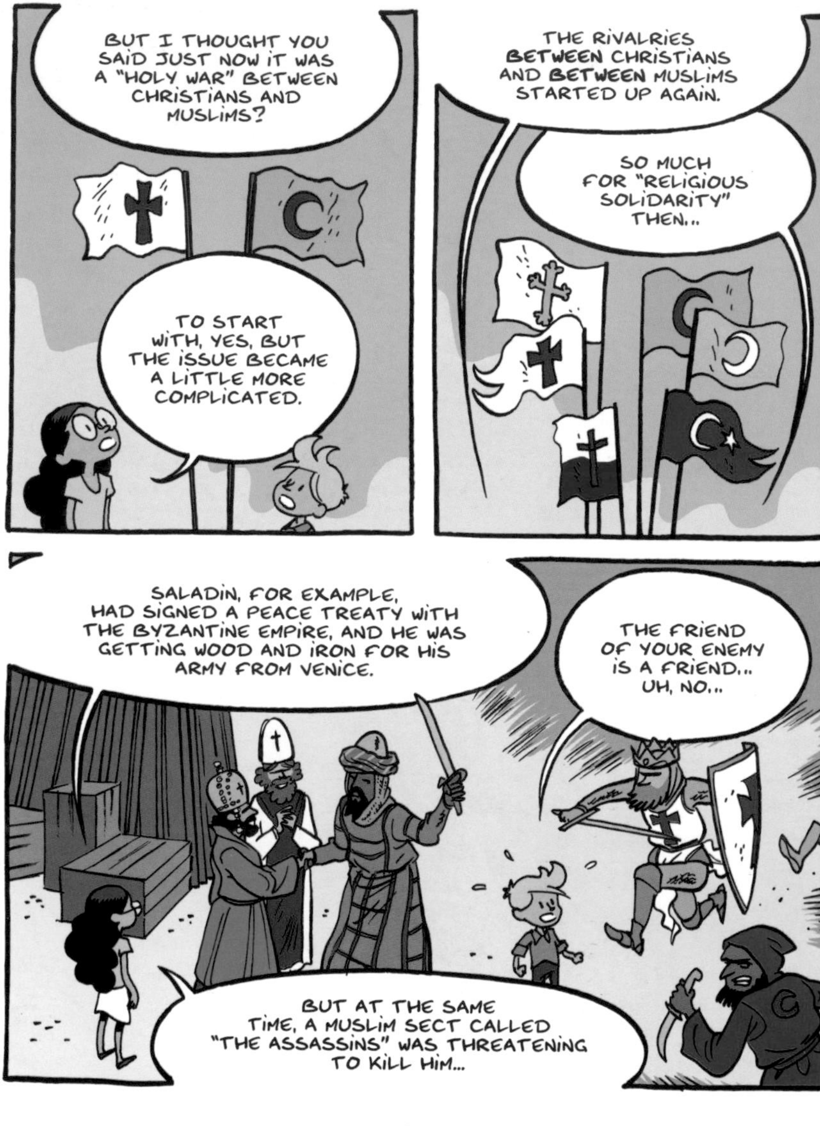
BUT I THOUGHT YOU SAID JUST NOW IT WAS A "HOLY WAR" BETWEEN CHRISTIANS AND MUSLIMS?
TO START WITH, YES, BUT THE ISSUE BECAME A LITTLE MORE COMPLICATED.
THE RIVALRIES **BETWEEN** CHRISTIANS AND **BETWEEN** MUSLIMS STARTED UP AGAIN.
SO MUCH FOR "RELIGIOUS SOLIDARITY" THEN...
SALADIN, FOR EXAMPLE, HAD SIGNED A PEACE TREATY WITH THE BYZANTINE EMPIRE, AND HE WAS GETTING WOOD AND IRON FOR HIS ARMY FROM VENICE.
THE FRIEND OF YOUR ENEMY IS A FRIEND... UH, NO...
BUT AT THE SAME TIME, A MUSLIM SECT CALLED "THE ASSASSINS" WAS THREATENING TO KILL HIM...

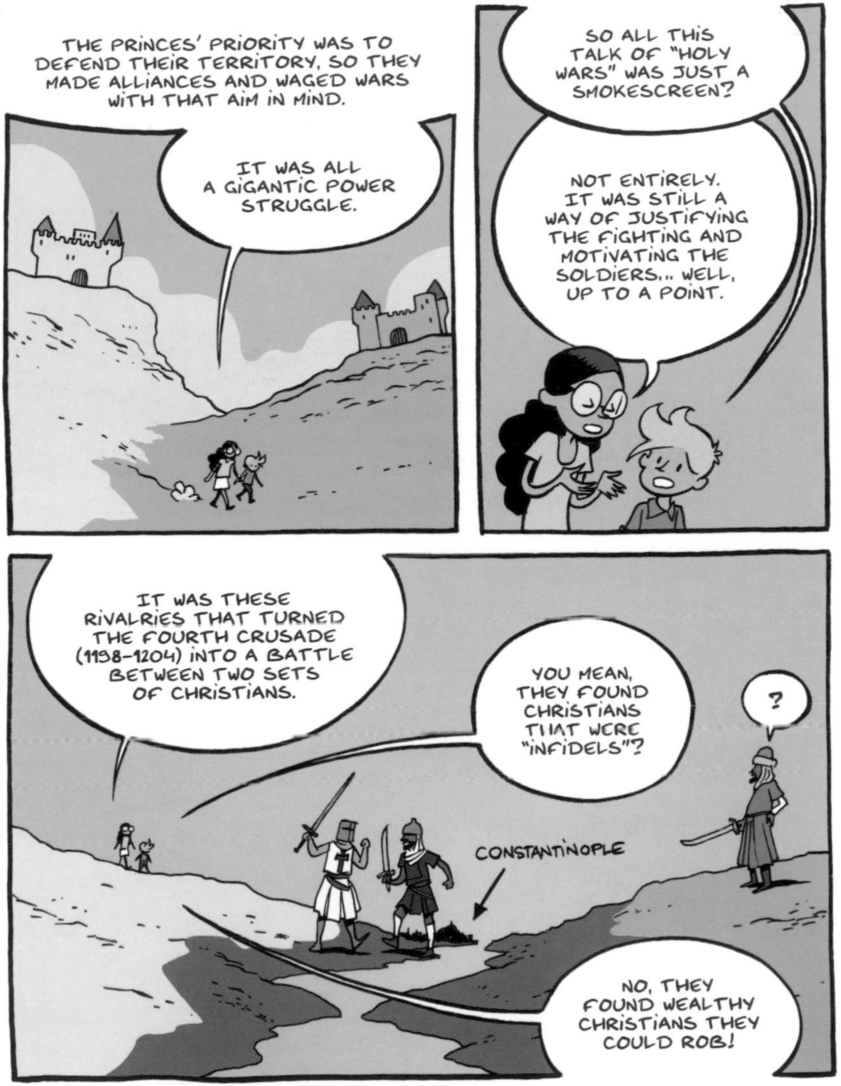
THE PRINCES' PRIORITY WAS TO DEFEND THEIR TERRITORY, SO THEY MADE ALLIANCES AND WAGED WARS WITH THAT AIM IN MIND.
IT WAS ALL A GIGANTIC POWER STRUGGLE.
SO ALL THIS TALK OF "HOLY WARS" WAS JUST A SMOKESCREEN?
NOT ENTIRELY. IT WAS STILL A WAY OF JUSTIFYING THE FIGHTING AND MOTIVATING THE SOLDIERS... WELL, UP TO A POINT.
IT WAS THESE RIVALRIES THAT TURNED THE FOURTH CRUSADE (1198–1204) INTO A BATTLE BETWEEN TWO SETS OF CHRISTIANS.
YOU MEAN, THEY FOUND CHRISTIANS THAT WERE "INFIDELS"?
?
CONSTANTINOPLE
NO, THEY FOUND WEALTHY CHRISTIANS THEY COULD ROB!

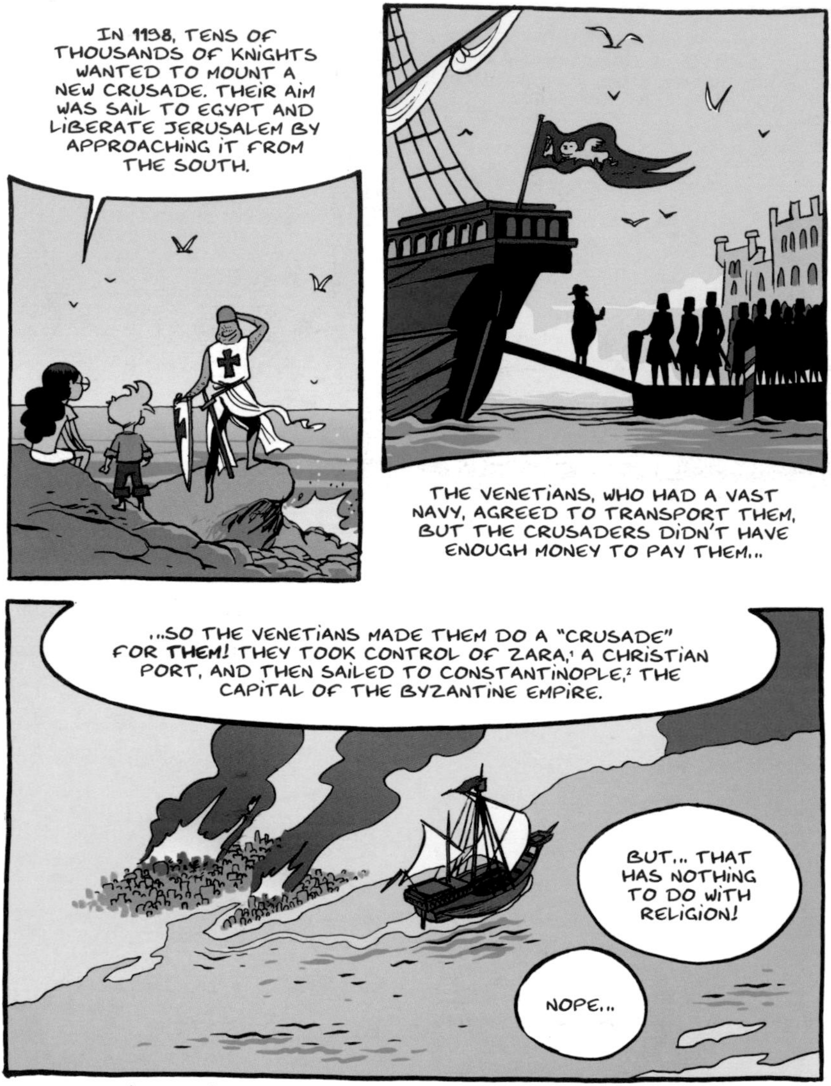
IN 1198, TENS OF THOUSANDS OF KNIGHTS WANTED TO MOUNT A NEW CRUSADE. THEIR AIM WAS SAIL TO EGYPT AND LIBERATE JERUSALEM BY APPROACHING IT FROM THE SOUTH.
THE VENETIANS, WHO HAD A VAST NAVY, AGREED TO TRANSPORT THEM, BUT THE CRUSADERS DIDN'T HAVE ENOUGH MONEY TO PAY THEM...
...SO THE VENETIANS MADE THEM DO A "CRUSADE" FOR **THEM!** THEY TOOK CONTROL OF ZARA,[1] A CHRISTIAN PORT, AND THEN SAILED TO CONSTANTINOPLE,[2] THE CAPITAL OF THE BYZANTINE EMPIRE.
BUT... THAT HAS NOTHING TO DO WITH RELIGION!
NOPE...

1. NOW ZADAR IN CROATIA.

2. NOW THE CAPITAL OF TURKEY, ISTANBUL.

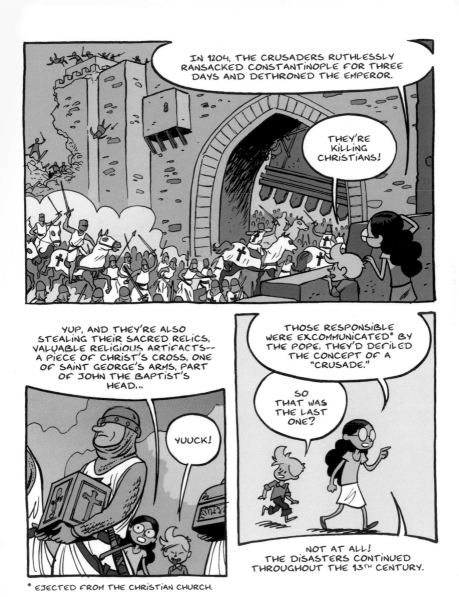

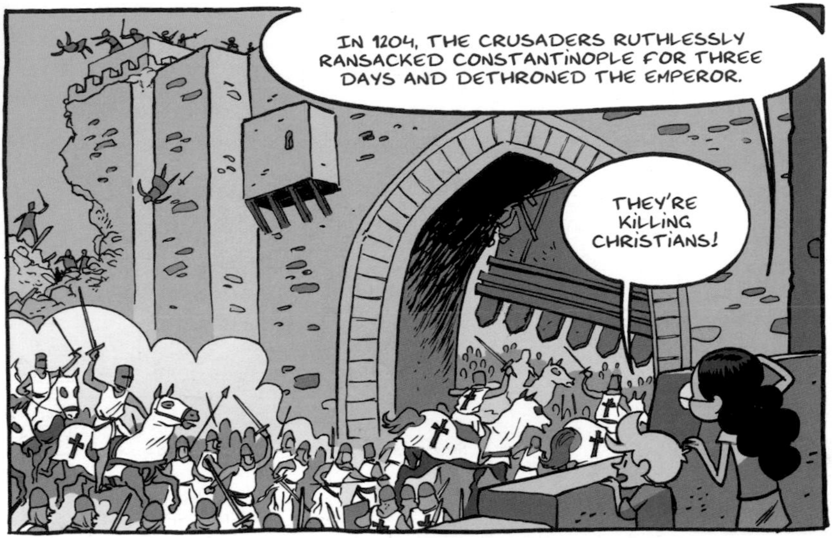
IN 1204, THE CRUSADERS RUTHLESSLY RANSACKED CONSTANTINOPLE FOR THREE DAYS AND DETHRONED THE EMPEROR.
THEY'RE KILLING CHRISTIANS!

YUP, AND THEY'RE ALSO STEALING THEIR SACRED RELICS, VALUABLE RELIGIOUS ARTIFACTS-- A PIECE OF CHRIST'S CROSS, ONE OF SAINT GEORGE'S ARMS, PART OF JOHN THE BAPTIST'S HEAD...

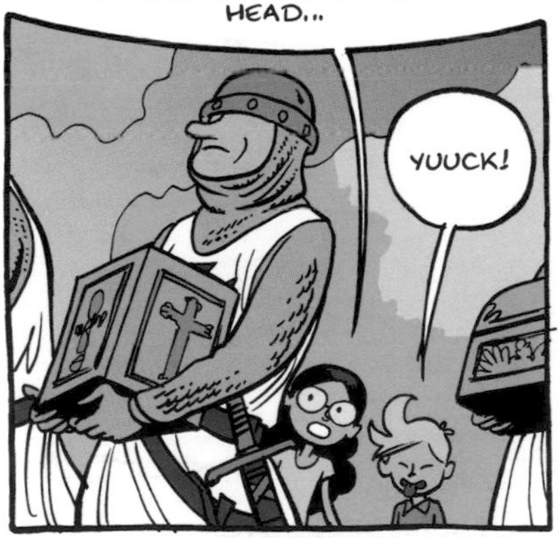
YUUCK!

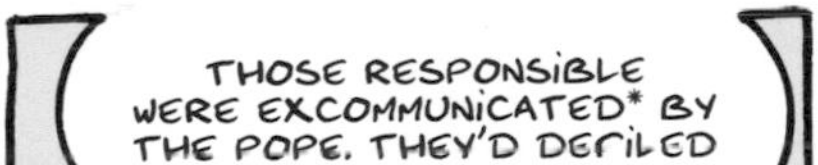
THOSE RESPONSIBLE WERE EXCOMMUNICATED* BY THE POPE. THEY'D DEFILED THE CONCEPT OF A "CRUSADE."
SO THAT WAS THE LAST ONE?

NOT AT ALL! THE DISASTERS CONTINUED THROUGHOUT THE 13TH CENTURY.

* EJECTED FROM THE CHRISTIAN CHURCH.

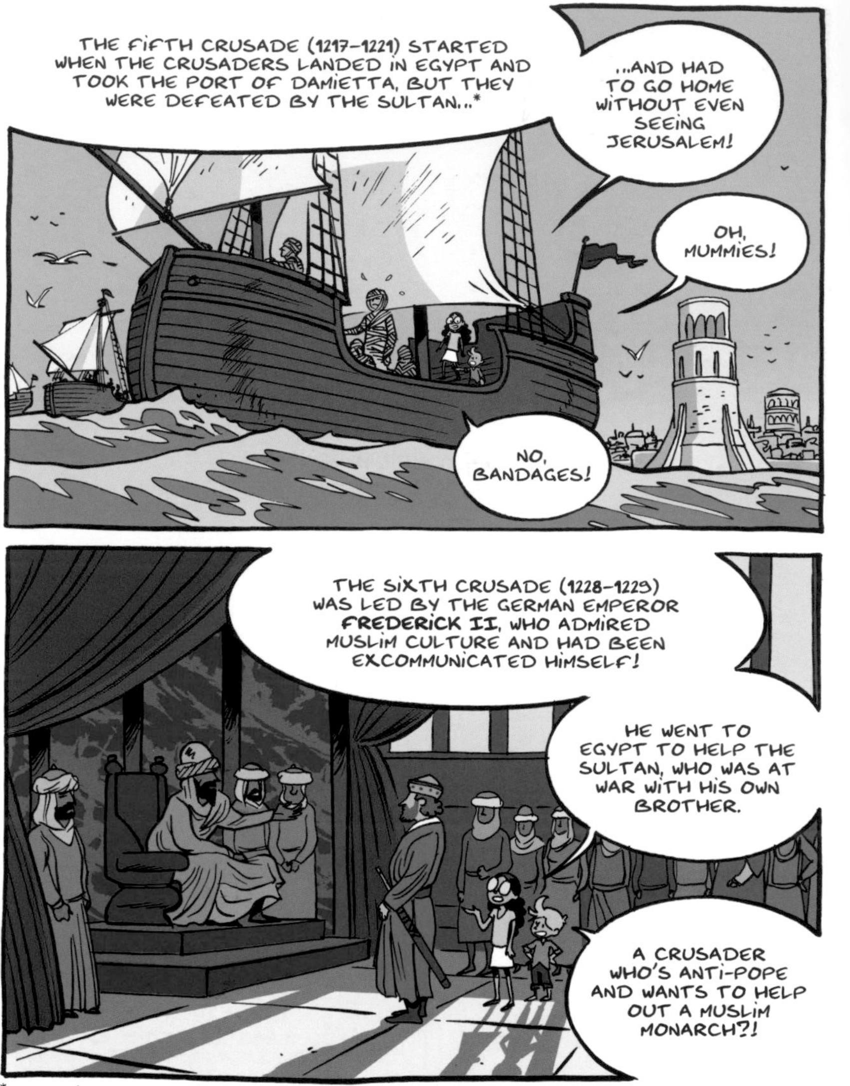
THE FiFTH CRUSADE (1217–1221) STARTED WHEN THE CRUSADERS LANDED IN EGYPT AND TOOK THE PORT OF DAMiETTA, BUT THEY WERE DEFEATED BY THE SULTAN...*
...AND HAD TO GO HOME WiTHOUT EVEN SEEING JERUSALEM!
OH, MUMMiES!
NO, BANDAGES!
THE SiXTH CRUSADE (1228–1229) WAS LED BY THE GERMAN EMPEROR **FREDERiCK II**, WHO ADMiRED MUSLiM CULTURE AND HAD BEEN EXCOMMUNiCATED HiMSELF!
HE WENT TO EGYPT TO HELP THE SULTAN, WHO WAS AT WAR WiTH HiS OWN BROTHER.
A CRUSADER WHO'S ANTi-POPE AND WANTS TO HELP OUT A MUSLiM MONARCH?!

* A MUSLiM RULER.

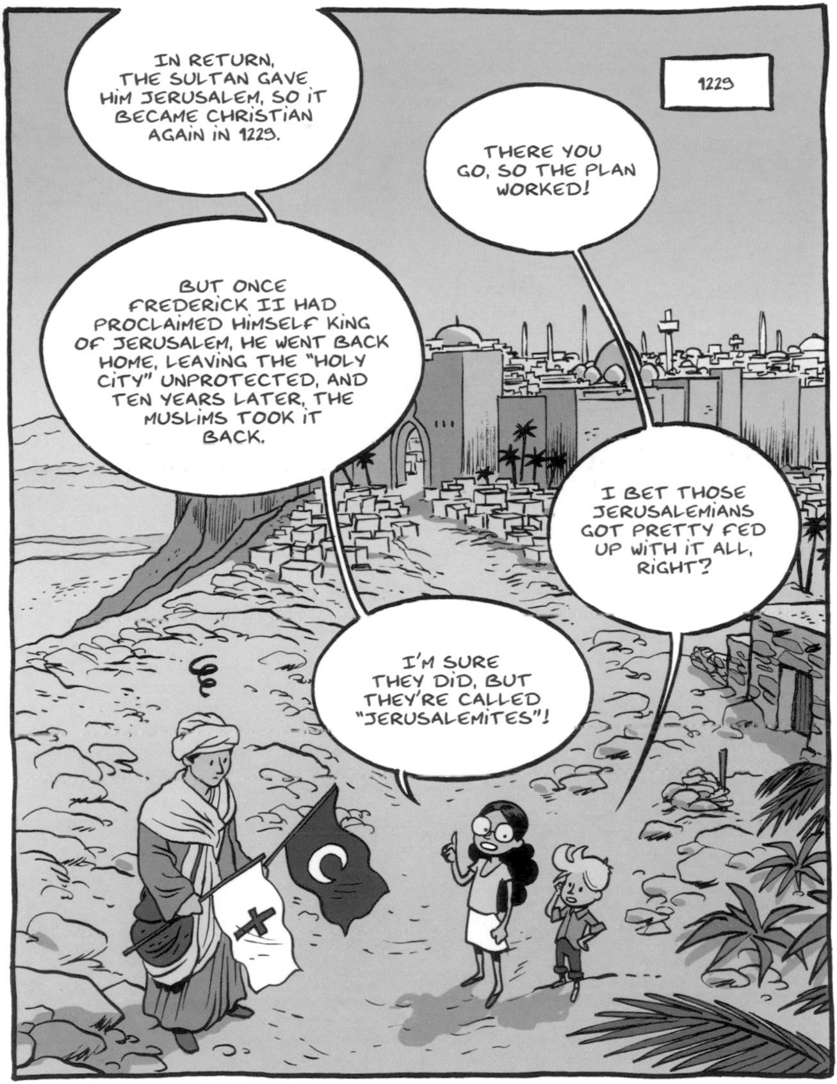
IN RETURN, THE SULTAN GAVE HIM JERUSALEM, SO IT BECAME CHRISTIAN AGAIN IN 1229.
1229
THERE YOU GO, SO THE PLAN WORKED!
BUT ONCE FREDERICK II HAD PROCLAIMED HIMSELF KING OF JERUSALEM, HE WENT BACK HOME, LEAVING THE "HOLY CITY" UNPROTECTED, AND TEN YEARS LATER, THE MUSLIMS TOOK IT BACK.
I BET THOSE JERUSALEMIANS GOT PRETTY FED UP WITH IT ALL, RIGHT?
I'M SURE THEY DID, BUT THEY'RE CALLED "JERUSALEMITES"!

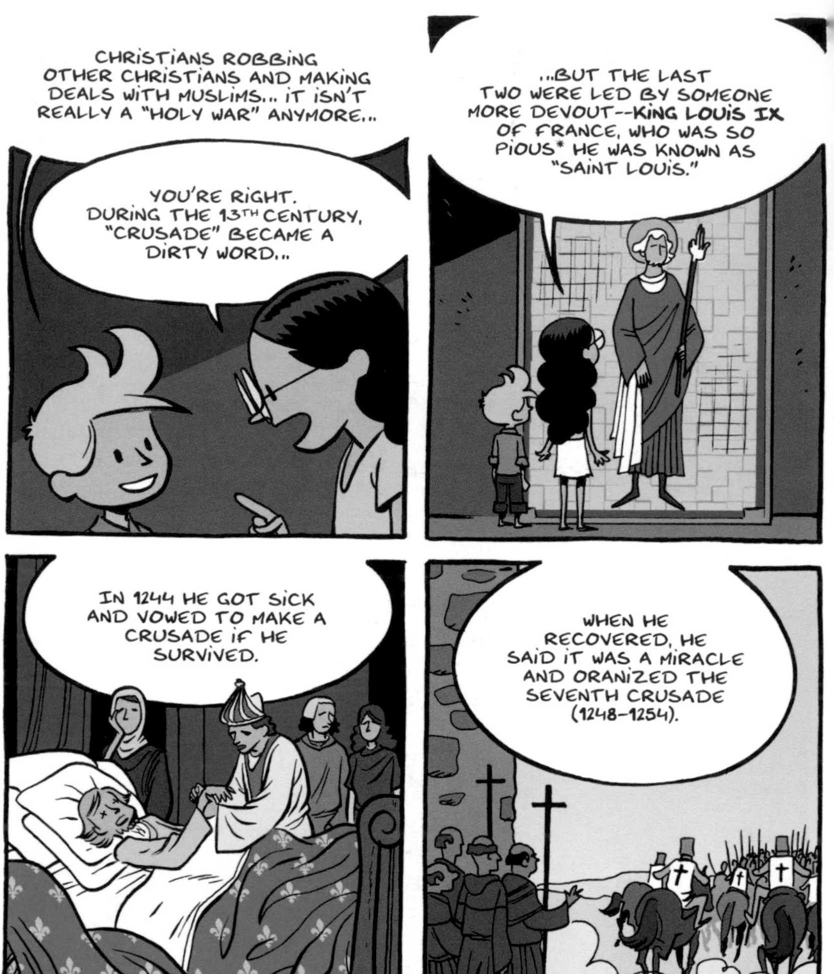
CHRISTIANS ROBBING OTHER CHRISTIANS AND MAKING DEALS WITH MUSLIMS... IT ISN'T REALLY A "HOLY WAR" ANYMORE...
YOU'RE RIGHT. DURING THE 13TH CENTURY, "CRUSADE" BECAME A DIRTY WORD...
...BUT THE LAST TWO WERE LED BY SOMEONE MORE DEVOUT--KING LOUIS IX OF FRANCE, WHO WAS SO PIOUS* HE WAS KNOWN AS "SAINT LOUIS."
IN 1244 HE GOT SICK AND VOWED TO MAKE A CRUSADE IF HE SURVIVED.
WHEN HE RECOVERED, HE SAID IT WAS A MIRACLE AND ORANIZED THE SEVENTH CRUSADE (1248–1254).

*DEVOUTLY RELIGIOUS.

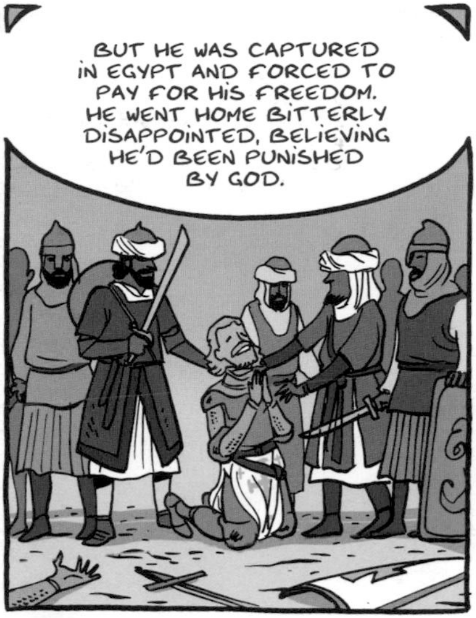
BUT HE WAS CAPTURED IN EGYPT AND FORCED TO PAY FOR HIS FREEDOM. HE WENT HOME BITTERLY DISAPPOINTED, BELIEVING HE'D BEEN PUNISHED BY GOD.

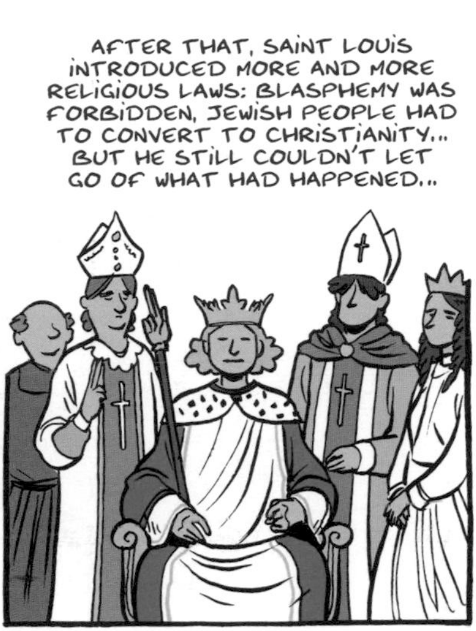
AFTER THAT, SAINT LOUIS INTRODUCED MORE AND MORE RELIGIOUS LAWS: BLASPHEMY WAS FORBIDDEN, JEWISH PEOPLE HAD TO CONVERT TO CHRISTIANITY... BUT HE STILL COULDN'T LET GO OF WHAT HAD HAPPENED...

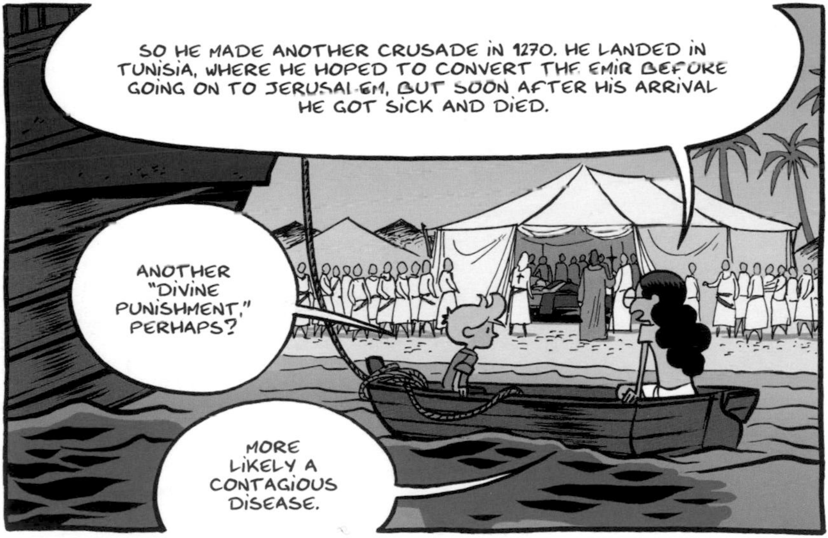
SO HE MADE ANOTHER CRUSADE IN 1270. HE LANDED IN TUNISIA, WHERE HE HOPED TO CONVERT THE EMIR BEFORE GOING ON TO JERUSALEM, BUT SOON AFTER HIS ARRIVAL HE GOT SICK AND DIED.
ANOTHER "DIVINE PUNISHMENT," PERHAPS?
MORE LIKELY A CONTAGIOUS DISEASE.

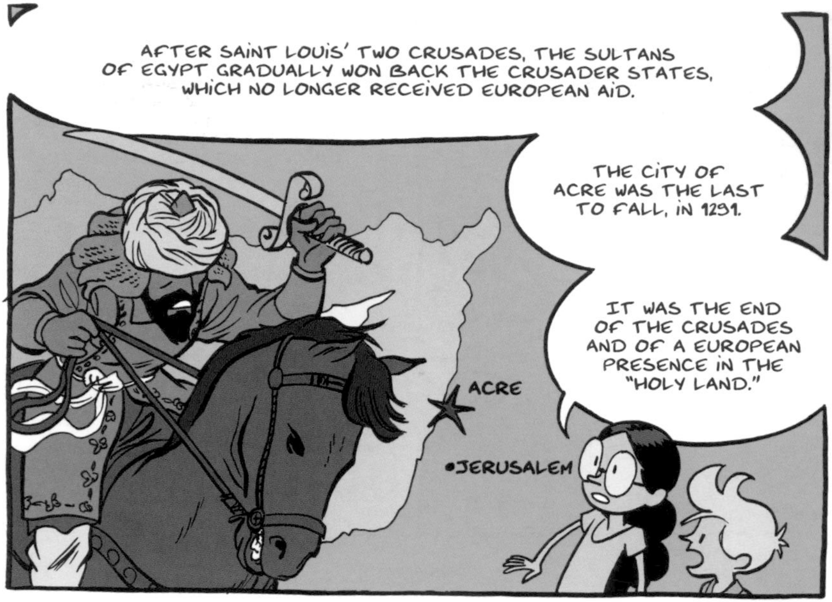
AFTER SAINT LOUIS' TWO CRUSADES, THE SULTANS OF EGYPT GRADUALLY WON BACK THE CRUSADER STATES, WHICH NO LONGER RECEIVED EUROPEAN AID.
THE CITY OF ACRE WAS THE LAST TO FALL, IN 1291.
IT WAS THE END OF THE CRUSADES AND OF A EUROPEAN PRESENCE IN THE "HOLY LAND."
ACRE
JERUSALEM

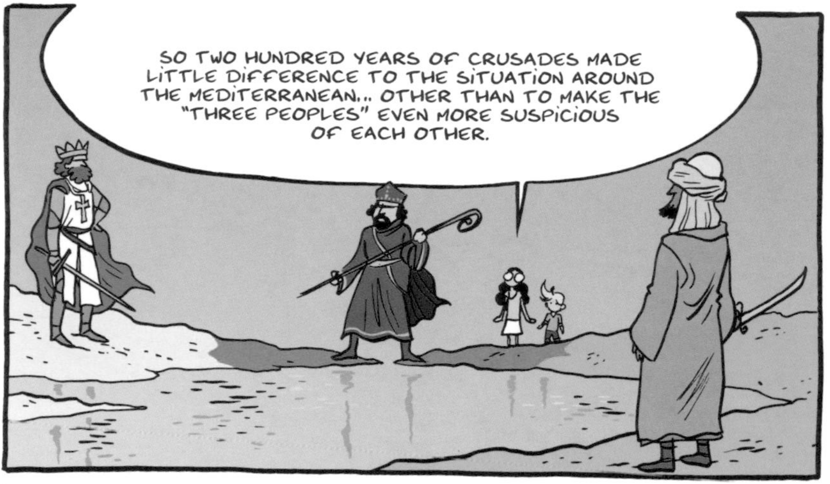
SO TWO HUNDRED YEARS OF CRUSADES MADE LITTLE DIFFERENCE TO THE SITUATION AROUND THE MEDITERRANEAN... OTHER THAN TO MAKE THE "THREE PEOPLES" EVEN MORE SUSPICIOUS OF EACH OTHER.

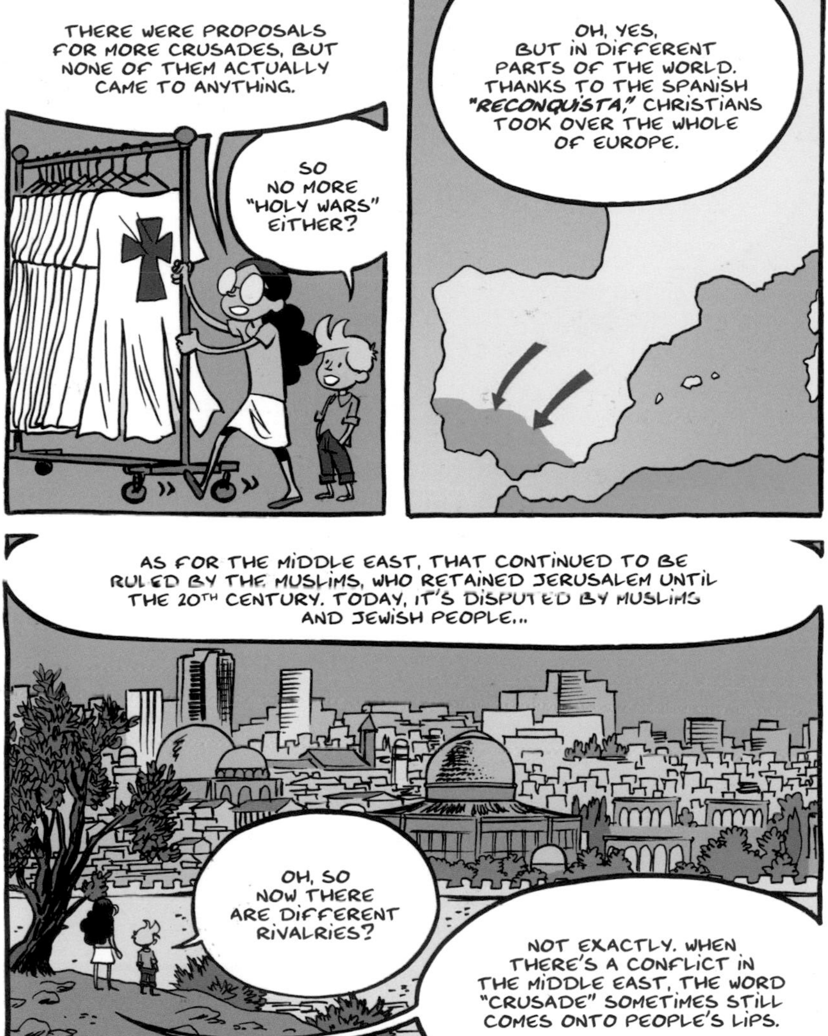
THERE WERE PROPOSALS FOR MORE CRUSADES, BUT NONE OF THEM ACTUALLY CAME TO ANYTHING.
SO NO MORE "HOLY WARS" EITHER?
OH, YES, BUT IN DIFFERENT PARTS OF THE WORLD. THANKS TO THE SPANISH *"RECONQUISTA,"* CHRISTIANS TOOK OVER THE WHOLE OF EUROPE.
AS FOR THE MIDDLE EAST, THAT CONTINUED TO BE RULED BY THE MUSLIMS, WHO RETAINED JERUSALEM UNTIL THE 20TH CENTURY. TODAY, IT'S DISPUTED BY MUSLIMS AND JEWISH PEOPLE...
OH, SO NOW THERE ARE DIFFERENT RIVALRIES?
NOT EXACTLY. WHEN THERE'S A CONFLICT IN THE MIDDLE EAST, THE WORD "CRUSADE" SOMETIMES STILL COMES ONTO PEOPLE'S LIPS.

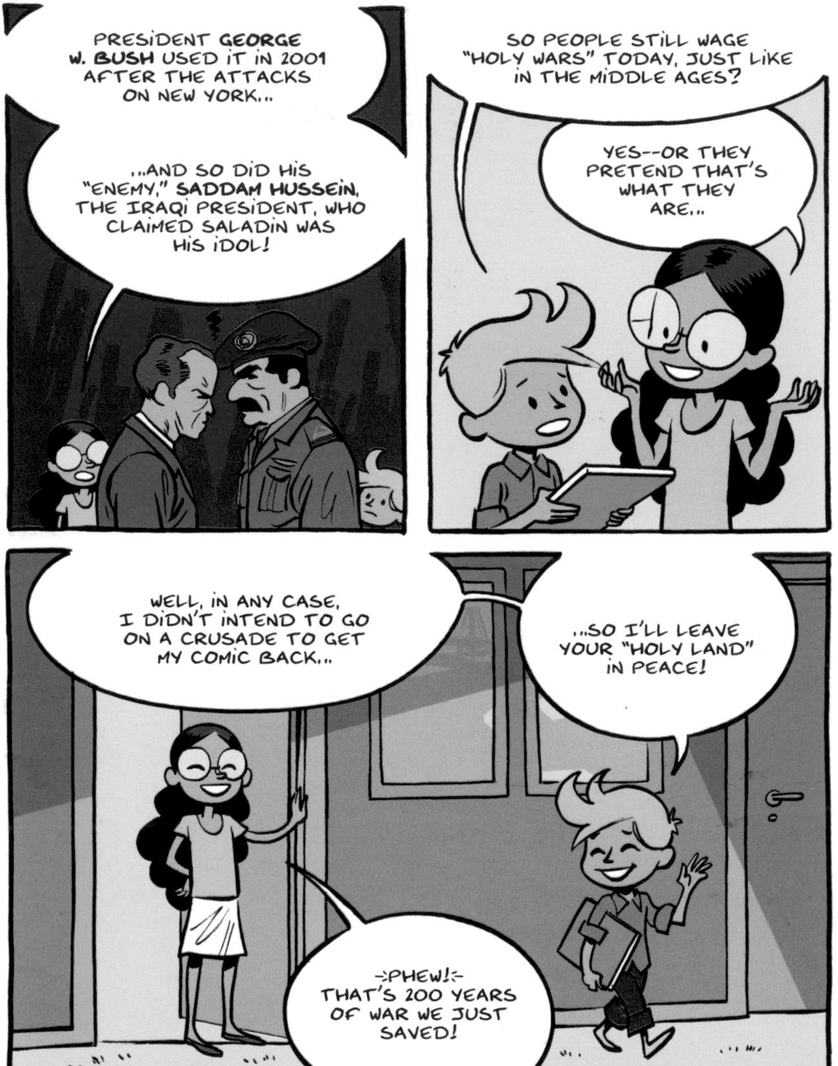
PRESIDENT GEORGE W. BUSH USED IT IN 2001 AFTER THE ATTACKS ON NEW YORK...
...AND SO DID HIS "ENEMY," SADDAM HUSSEIN, THE IRAQI PRESIDENT, WHO CLAIMED SALADIN WAS HIS IDOL!
SO PEOPLE STILL WAGE "HOLY WARS" TODAY, JUST LIKE IN THE MIDDLE AGES?
YES--OR THEY PRETEND THAT'S WHAT THEY ARE...
WELL, IN ANY CASE, I DIDN'T INTEND TO GO ON A CRUSADE TO GET MY COMIC BACK...
...SO I'LL LEAVE YOUR "HOLY LAND" IN PEACE!
PHEW!
THAT'S 200 YEARS OF WAR WE JUST SAVED!

And there's more...

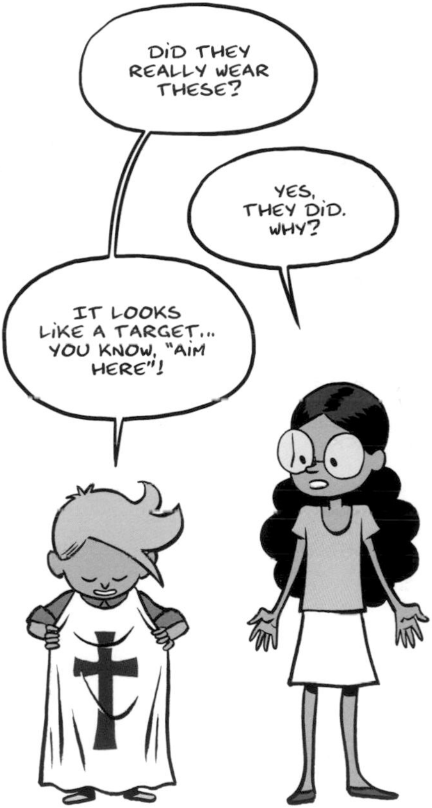
DID THEY REALLY WEAR THESE?
YES, THEY DID. WHY?
IT LOOKS LIKE A TARGET... YOU KNOW, "AIM HERE"!

Some people who made history

Godfrey of Bouillon
(c. 1060–1100)

A descendant of Charlemagne, Godfrey of Bouillon was one of the leaders of the First Crusade. He sold his estates to raise an army and crossed Europe to reach the "Holy Land." Arriving in Jerusalem in 1099, he ordered it to be attacked and both Muslim and Jewish citizens to be massacred. He then became "Defender of the Holy Sepulchre" — in other words, ruler of the new Kingdom of Jerusalem. He died a year later, possibly poisoned by a pinecone.

Richard the Lionheart
(1157–1199)

Although he was the King of England, Richard the Lionheart spent most of his time defending his possessions in France, which he'd inherited from his mother, Eleanor of Aquitaine. He led the Third Crusade with his rival King Philippe Auguste of France, and challenged him constantly, earning the nickname "Lionheart." He returned to the East in 1192 after signing a peace treaty with Saladin, and he died while beseiging the *Château de Châlus-Charbol* in 1199.

Saladin
(1138–1193)

One of a large Kurdish family, Saladin succeeded his uncle as ruler of Egypt in 1169. He promptly conquered Syria and part of Iraq, bringing the Muslims together by declaring a "*jihad*." He stood against the Crusaders and crushed them at the Battle of Hattin in 1187, after which he retook Jerusalem. He then repelled the Third Crusade, which had set out to defeat him. Founder of the Ayyubid dynasty, Saladin is regarded as a hero by Muslims.

Baibars
(1223–1277)

A former slave who became one of the Sultan's bodyguards, Baibars eventually ruled Egypt, joining the list of *Mamluk* (slave) sultans. Determined to win back the territories lost to the Crusaders, he fought against Saint Louis during the Seventh Crusade and took him prisoner in 1250. After several other victories, he succeeded in taking the *Krak des Chevaliers* fortress in Syria in 1271, at the end of the last Crusade.

West meets East

In the Middle Ages, the Arab world in the East was in many ways more advanced than the Christian world in the West. Thanks to the Crusades, Europeans exchanged ideas and made many advances.

Eastern delights

Sugar: During the First Crusade, Europeans came across plantations of "sweet salt" in Syria. This was sugar cane — then unknown in the West. As well as enjoying the cakes and candies that were made from it, they recognized the importance of its use in medicine.

Sugar cane being crushed in a mill

The astrolabe: This was a device used by Arab astrologers to determine the height of stars above the horizon. Adapting it as a tool for navigation, European explorers subsequently used it to cross the world's oceans.

The compass: Invented in China, the compass reached Europe in the 12th century — probably via the Middle East.

The zero: First used in India, the zero ("*sifr*" in Arabic, meaning "empty") was adopted by Europeans around 1120 thanks to the translation of a treatise written by **al-Khwarizmi** by the English scholar **Adelard of Bath**, who had lived in Syria.

Travel and trade

The start of passenger travel:
Most pilgrims — and there were
increasing numbers of them —
traveled by boat. In the 13th century,
3,000 people were transported
from Marseille each year by just two
ships. All this boosted the eco-
nomy: in 1248, **Guy de Forez** had to
pay 975 marcs to transport troops
to the East — that's
530 pounds of silver!

**The cog — a supply and troop
ship used by the Knights Templar**

The rise of the Italian market towns:
International trade wasn't restricted by
the Holy Wars. On the
contrary, in the 13th century, almost
half of Genoa's trade was with Syria
and Egypt, while Venice developed
a trading "empire" around the Mediterranean and the Black Sea that lasted
400 years.

international transfers: Not only trade,
but also the payment of ransoms to free
prisoners during the Crusades increased
the international circulation of money;
and the banking system developed out
of money-lending and the use of bills of
exchange (what we now call checks).

**An Italian
merchant ship**

39

Crusader troops

Cavalry

Mounted soldiers, generally following their prince, came from all over Europe to fight the "infidels." The "Code of Chivalry" (from the French *"cheval,"* meaning "horse") demanded bravery, especially in religious battles.

Infantry

Foot soldiers followed the cavalry and tried to disarm their opponents with a club or guisarme (a pole used for knocking men off horses). There were usually between 7 and 12 infantry for each cavalry soldier.

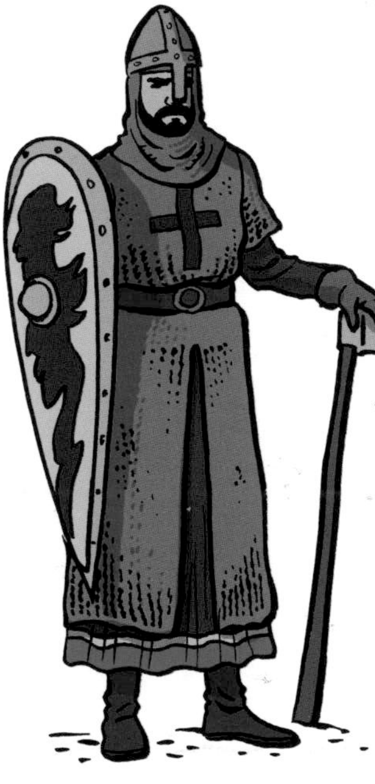

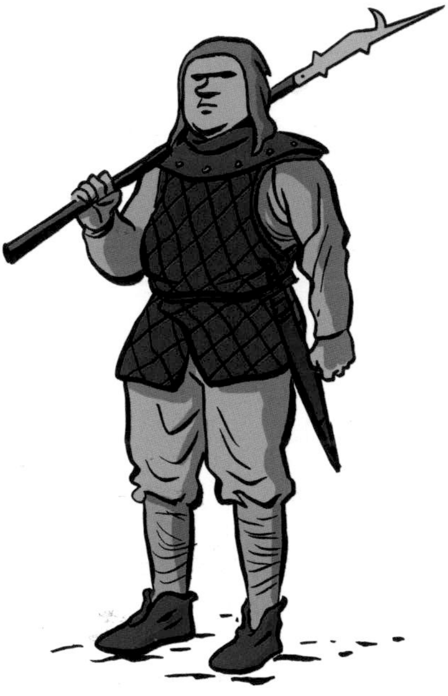

Knights Templar

The Knights Templar protected both pilgrims and sacred shrines. After the loss of the Crusader States, they returned to Europe, where they became so powerful that **Philip IV of France** disbanded them in 1307.

Turcopoles

Turcopoles were Eastern mercenaries, mostly Christian Turks, who fought for the Crusaders. The Muslims regarded them as traitors — those who were captured at Hattin by Saladin were executed.

Timeline

The Turks take Jerusalem and forbid Christian pilgrims to visit.

▼

1078

Pope Urban II's "appeal" from Clermont-Ferrand launches the First Crusade.

▼

1095

1219

▲

Damietta, in Egypt, falls to the Europeans during the Fifth Crusade.

1204

▲

Constantinople is sacked during the Fourth Crusade.

1229

▲

The German Emperor, Frederick II, wins Jerusalem back during the Sixth Crusade.

1250

▲

Saint Louis is taken prisoner during the Sixth Crusade.

The Crusaders take Jerusalem.

The Turks win back Edessa.

Bernard calls for a Second Crusade.

1099

1144

1146

1192

1187

An agreement between Saladin and Richard the Lionheart ends the Third Crusade.

The Crusaders are defeated at the Battle of Hattin by Saladin, who retakes Jerusalem.

1270

1291

Saint Louis dies of illness in Tunis during the Eighth Crusade.

Acre, last bastion of Christendom in the Holy Land, falls and the Crusades end.

WATCH OUT FOR PAPERCUT**Z**

Welcome to the fearlessly fanatical fourth MAGICAL HISTORY TOUR graphic novel, this one focused on "The Crusades and the Holy Wars," exhaustively researched and written by Fabrice Erre and illustrated by Sylvain Savoia, from Papercutz, those zealots dedicated to publishing great graphic novels for all ages. I'm Jim Salicrup, the Editor-in-Chief and Peace-loving Infidel here to share a few thoughts regarding the Holy Wars…

A few years back I was fortunate to travel to Granada, Spain as a guest at a comics convention. My hosts were extremely generous and went out of their way to entertain both invited guests and convention attendees. One of the perks was a guided tour of Alhambra, a palace and fortress complex. While many of my fellow guests were marveling at the architectural beauty of the place, I couldn't help feeling depressed by its war-torn history. This place was in many ways a monument to the never-ending conflicts between Christians and Muslims, dating back centuries. We were guided through a dungeon here and a fortress there, and all I could think of was why would anyone fight in such a beautiful country? Wouldn't it be better to just enjoy this wonderful land together?

That's not to say that only Christians and Muslims ever fought wars, unfortunately there have been wars all throughout history and it continues to this day. I guess what depressed me so was the overall pointlessness of it all. I mean, after literally centuries of fighting nothing really has been resolved in a manner that satisfies everyone, and even today, many of the basic disputes are still not settled. Despite the messages of peace and love found in most religions, people continue to wage holy wars.

It's funny, I also was fortunate enough to attend a comics convention in Moscow, Russia, and what I discovered was the comics fans in Russia were very much like the comics fans in Spain who were very much like the comics fans in North America. It seems crazy that people from all over can easily get along and share their common interests together, yet our governments struggle to maintain peaceful relationships with each other.

The conventional thinking is that perhaps if we study history, we can avoid making the mistakes of the past. That may just be another benefit of reading MAGICAL HISTORY TOUR. By publishing this graphic novel series, Papercutz is doing our part to contribute to world peace.

Thanks,

JIM

© Editions du Seuil, 1995

Did you know one of the editors of MAGICAL HISTORY TOUR is also an award-winning cartoonist? It's true! And Papercutz will soon be publishing one of Lewis Trondheim's comic art masterpieces THE FLY.

© Editions du Seuil, 1995

STAY IN TOUCH!

EMAIL: salicrup@papercutz.com
WEB: www.papercutz.com
TWITTER: @papercutzgn
INSTAGRAM: @papercutzgn
FACEBOOK: PAPERCUTZGRAPHICNOVELS
FANMAIL: Papercutz, 160 Broadway, Suite 700, East Wing, New York, NY 10038

Go to papercutz.com and sign up for the free Papercutz e-newsletter!

Fabrice Erre has a Ph.D. in History and teaches Geography and History at the *Lycee Jean Jaures* near Montpellier, France. He has written a thesis on the satirical press, writes the blog *Une annee au lycee (A Year in High School)* on the website of *Le Monde*, one of France's top national newspapers, and has published several comics.

Sylvain Savoia draws the *Marzi* series, which tells the history of Poland as seen through the eyes of a child. He has also drawn *Les esclaves oublies de Tromelin (The Forgotten Slaves of Tromelin)*, which won the *Academie de Marine de Paris* prize.

MORE GREAT GRAPHIC NOVEL
SERIES AVAILABLE FROM
PAPERCUTZ™

THE SMURFS TALES #1

BRINA THE CAT #1

CAT & CAT #1

THE SISTERS #1

ATTACK OF THE STUFF

ASTERIX #1

THE LOUD HOUSE #1

LOLA'S SUPER CLUB #1

THE MYTHICS #1

GUMBY #1

MELOWY #1

BLUEBEARD

DINOSAUR EXPLORERS #1

THE LITTLE MERMAID

FUZZY DAOBBALL #1

ASTRO MOUSE
AND LIGHT BULB #1

GERONIMO STILTON
REPORTER #1

SCHOOL FOR EXTRA-
TERRESTRIAL GIRLS #1

X-VENTURE
XPLORERS #1

THE ONLY LIVING
GIRL #1

papercutz.com
Also available where ebooks are sold.

Melowy, Geronimo Stilton; © 2018 Atlantyca S.p.A; Bluebeard, The Little Mermaid © 2018 Metaphrog; Fuzzy Baseball © 2018 by John Steven Gurney; The Loud House © 2018 Viacom International Inc.; The Only Living Girl © 2018-2019 Bottled Lightening LLC.; GUMBY ©2018 Prema Toy Co., Inc.; The Sisters, Cat & Cat © 2018 BAMBOO ÉDITION; Brina the Cat © 2020 TUNUÉ (Tunué s.r.l.); Attack of the Stuff © 2020, Jim Benton; The Mythics © 2020 Éditions Delcourt. ASTERIX® - OBELIX ® - IDEFIX ® -DOGMATIX ®© 2020 HACHETTE LIVRE. Astro Mouse and Light Bulb © 2020 Bang Editions and Fermín Solís. Lola's Super Club ©Christine Beigel + Pierrer Fouillet, Bang Editions. Dinosaur Explorers and X-Venture Explorers © 2021 Kodakowa Gempak Starz; School for Extraterrestrial Girls © 2020 Jeremy Whitley and Jamie Noguchi. - 2018 - Licensed through I.M.P.S. (Brussels) - www.smurf.com

WHERE WILL THE MAGICAL HISTORY TOUR BRING ANNIE AND NICO NEXT?

MAGICAL HISTORY TOUR graphic novels are available in hardcover only for $6.99 each at booksellers everywhere. Order online at www.papercutz.com.
Or call 1-800-886-1223,
Monday through Friday, 9 – 5 EST. MC, Visa, and AmEx accepted.
To order by mail, please add $5.00 for postage and handling for first book ordered, $1.00 for each additional book and make check payable to NBM Publishing.
Send to: Papercutz, 160 Broadway, Suite 700, East Wing, New York, NY 10038.

MAGICAL HISTORY TOUR graphic novels are also available digitally wherever e-books are sold.